LION
COLORING BOOK
FOR ADULTS

AN ADULT COLORING BOOK OF 40 LIONS IN A RANGE OF STYLES AND ORNATE PATTERNS

ADULT COLORING WORLD

Copyright © 2015 Adult Coloring World

All rights reserved.

ISBN-13: 978-1519699671

ISBN-10: 1519699670

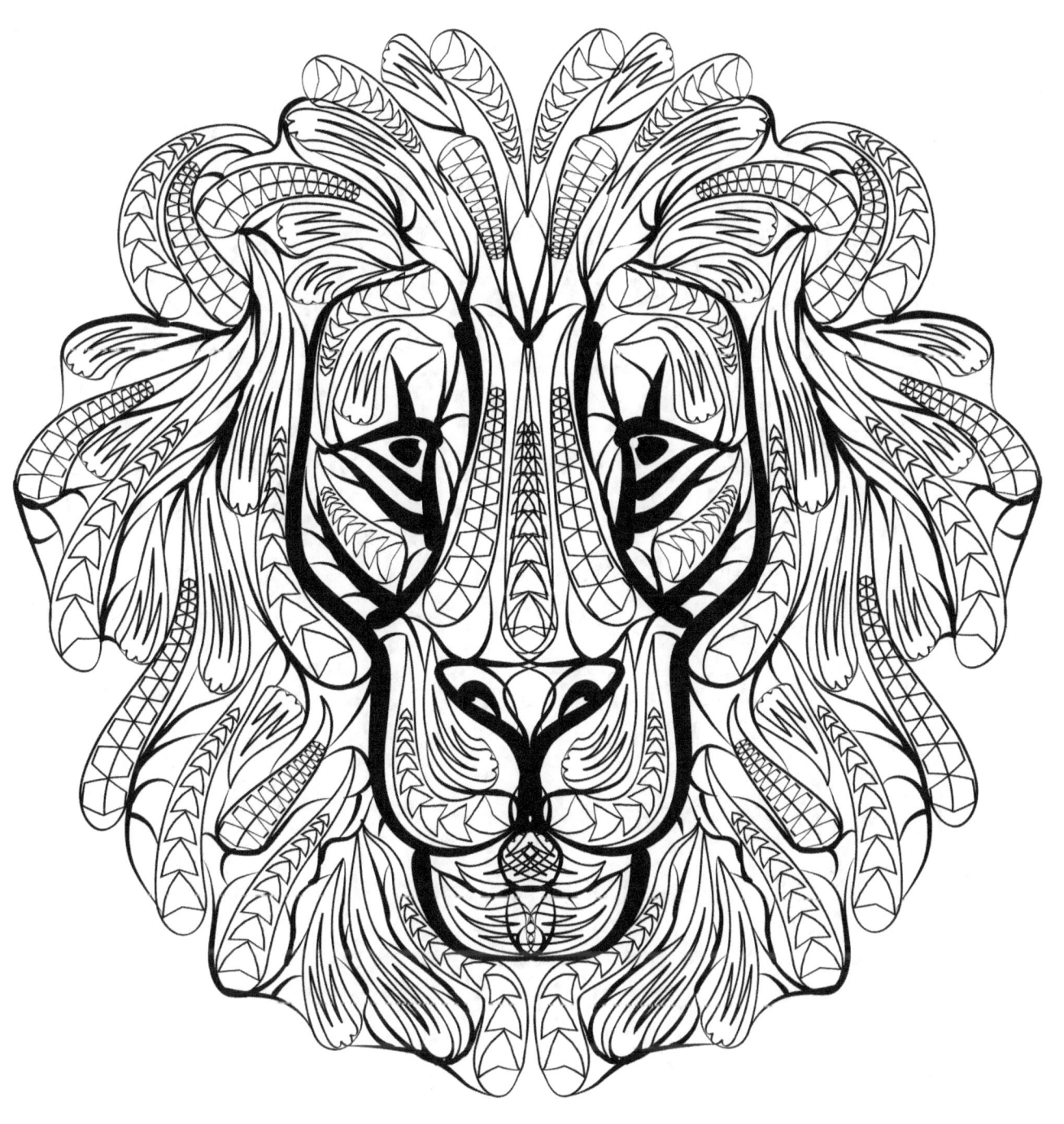

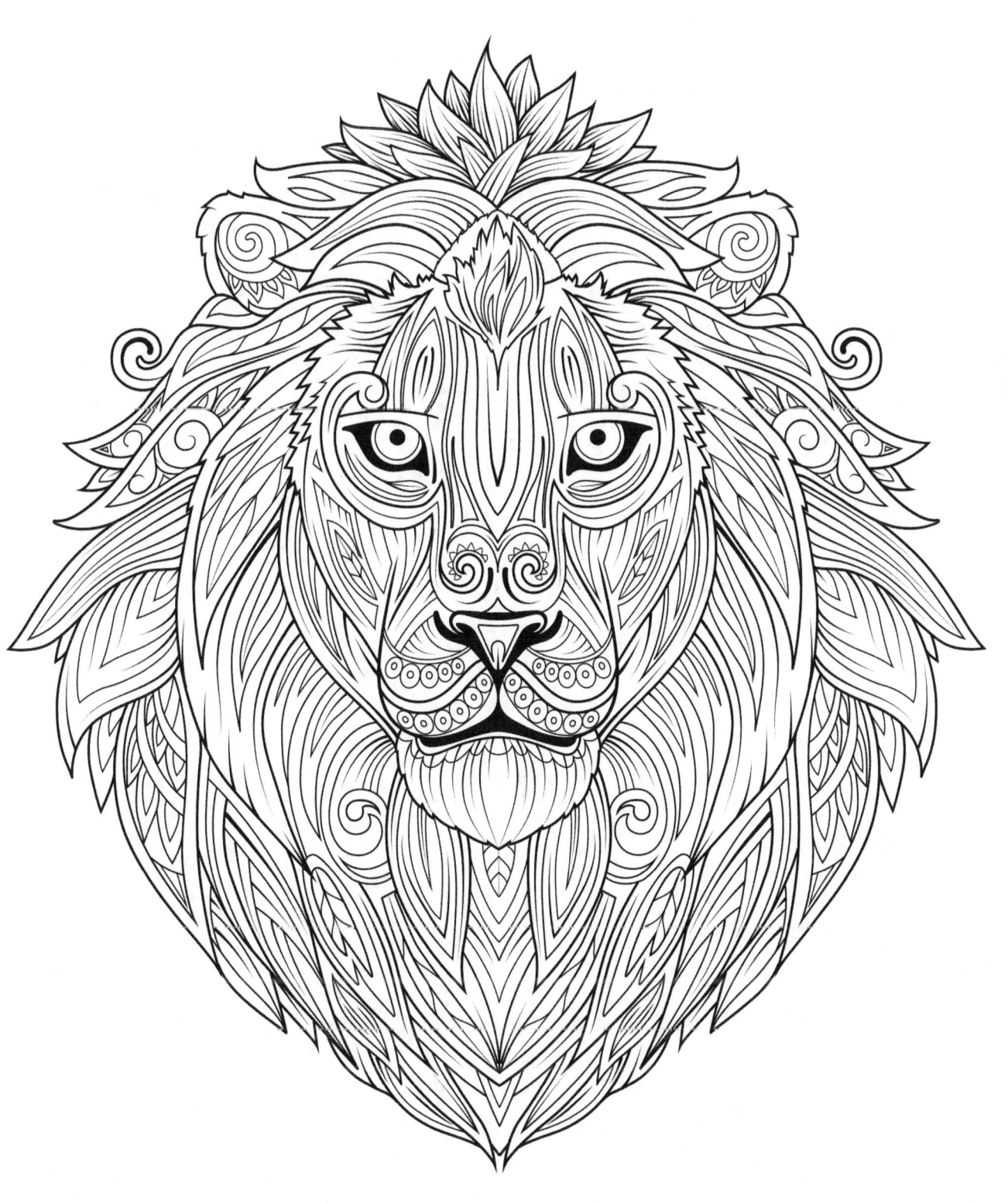

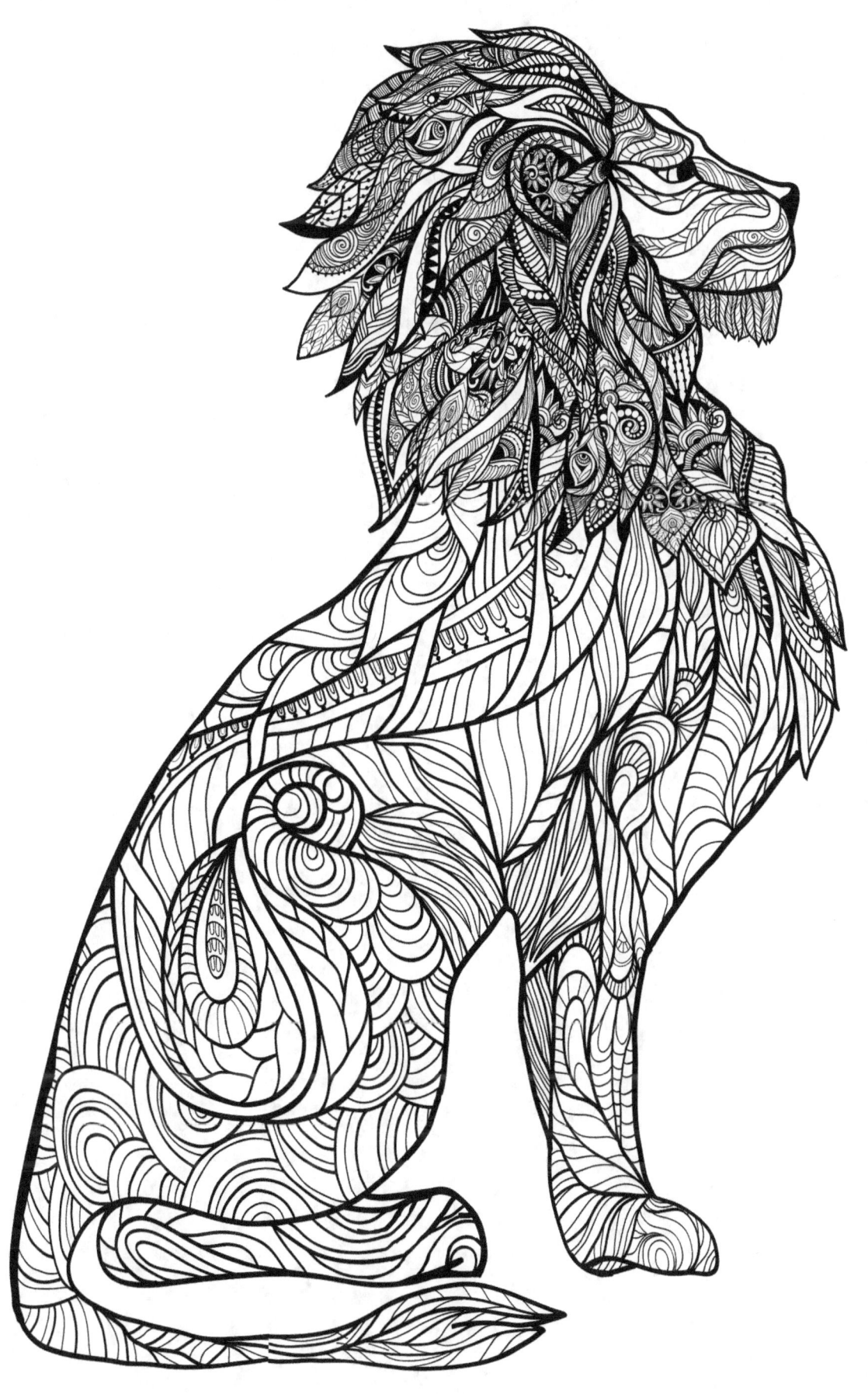

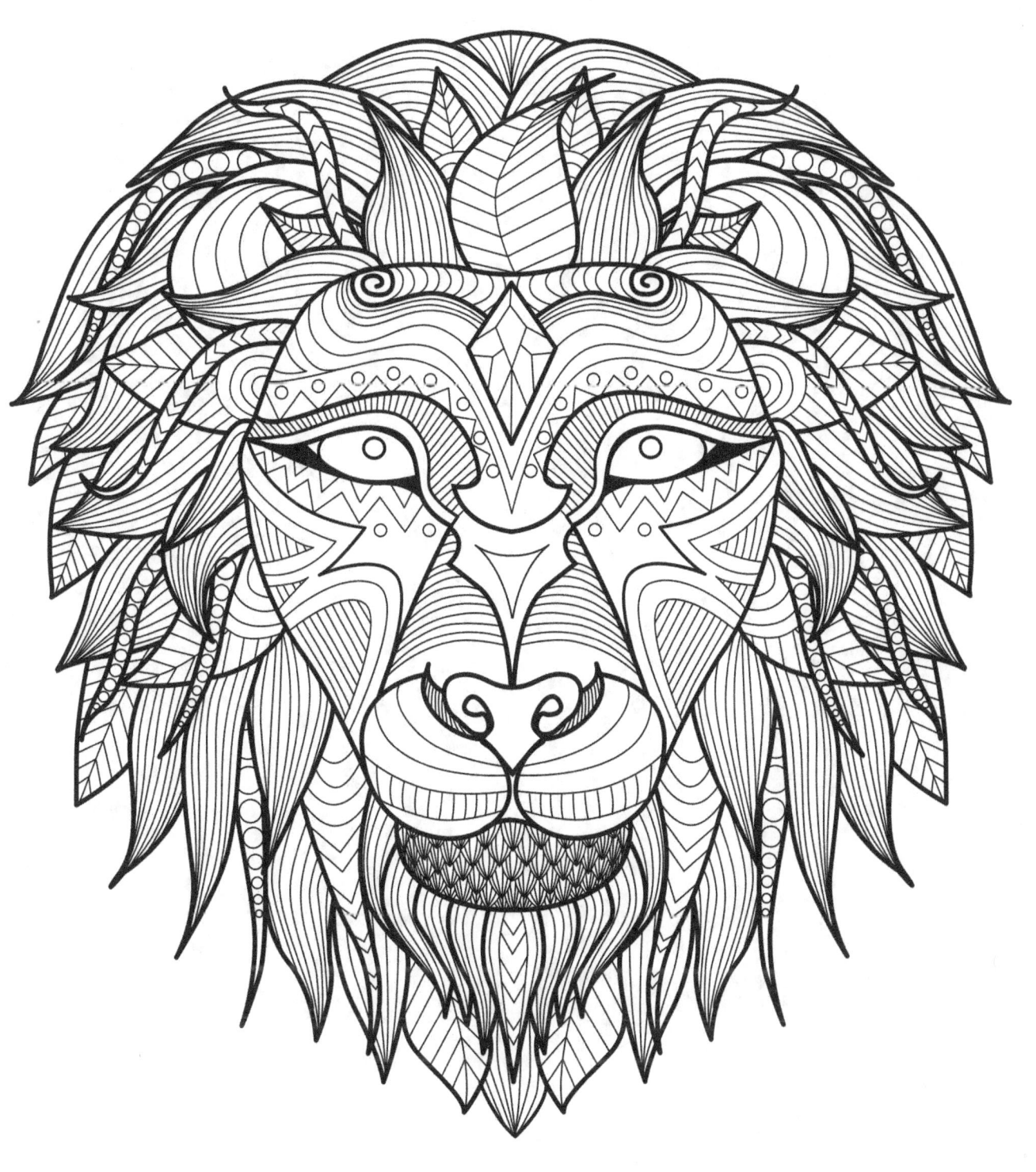

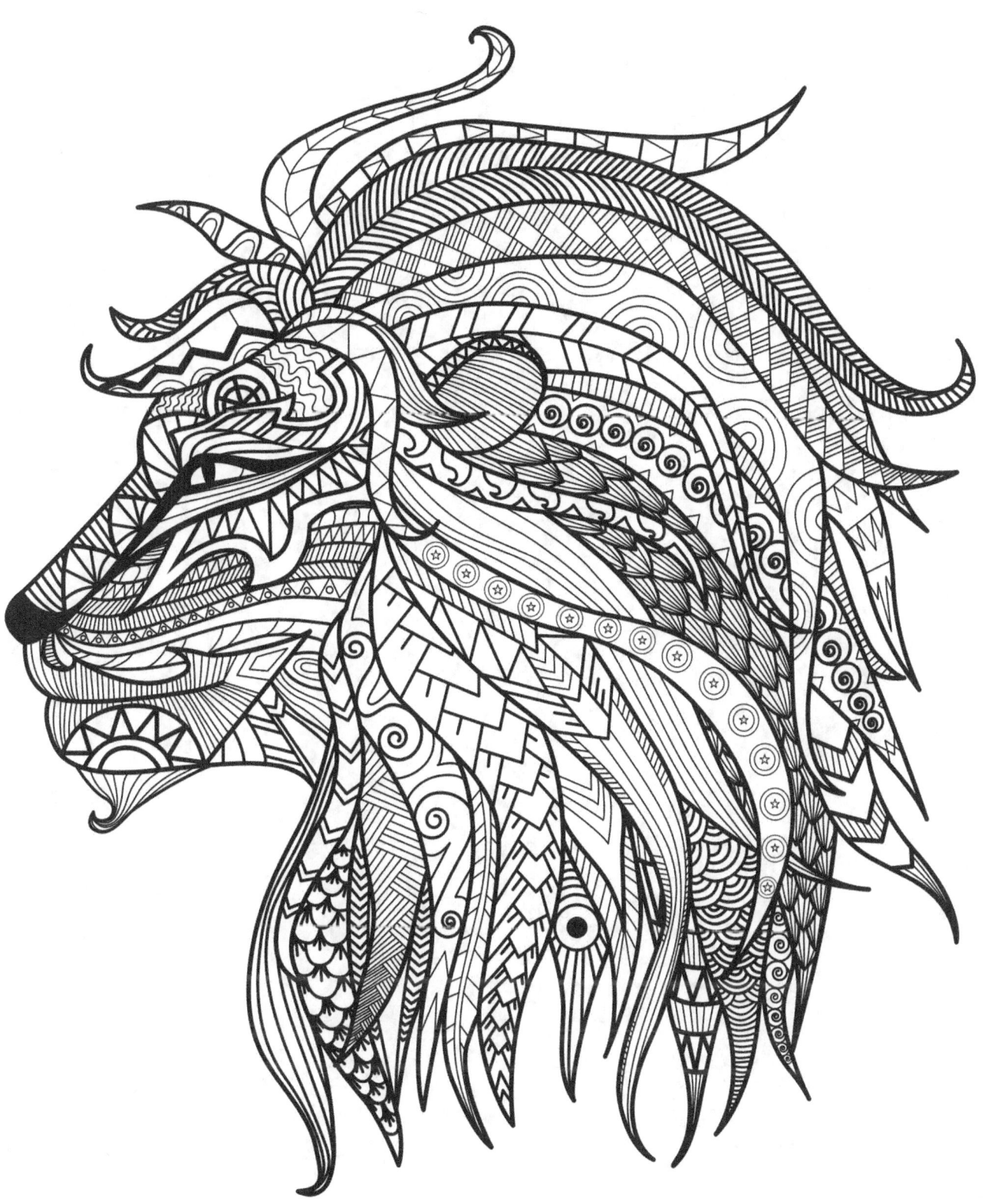

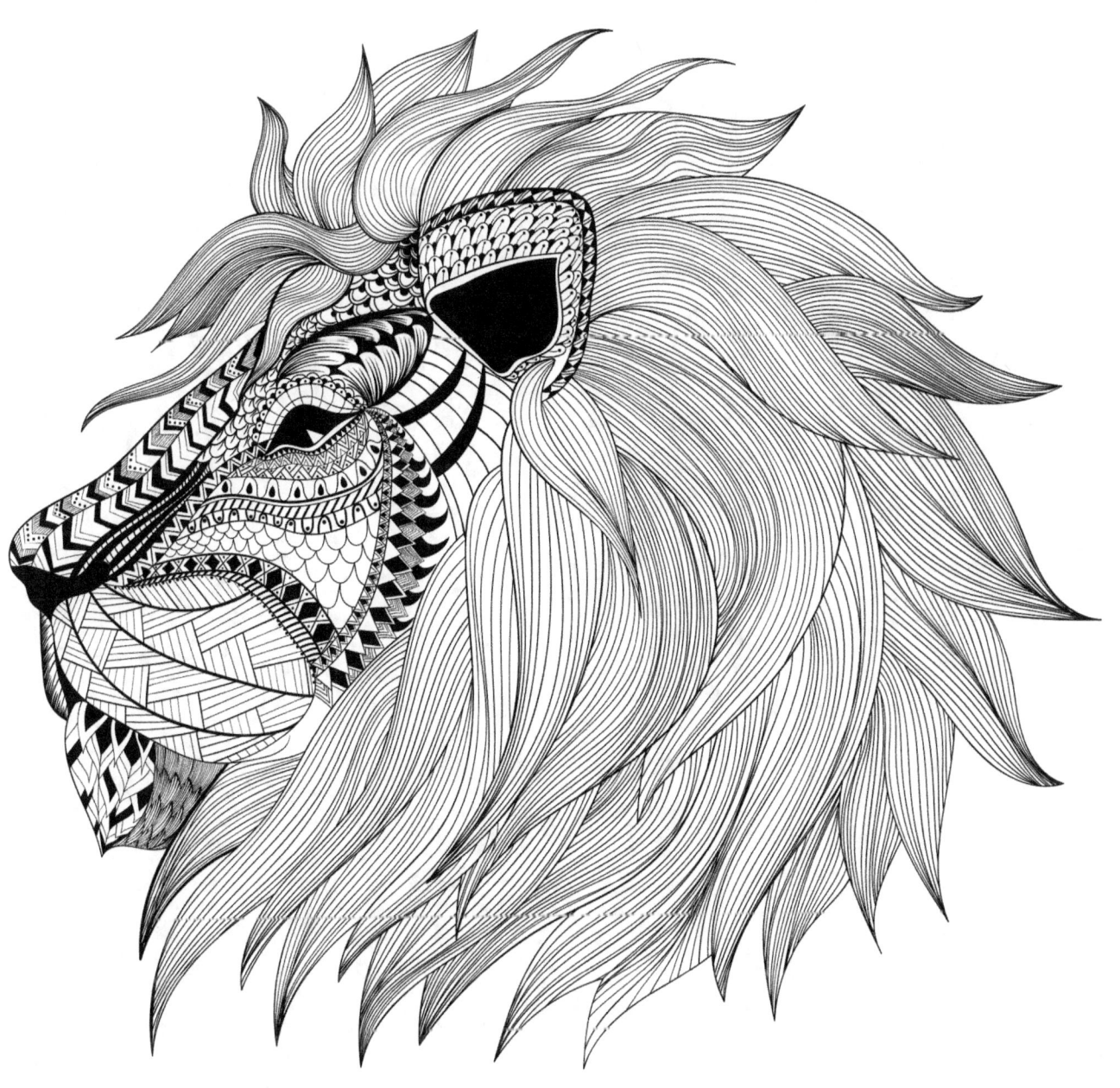

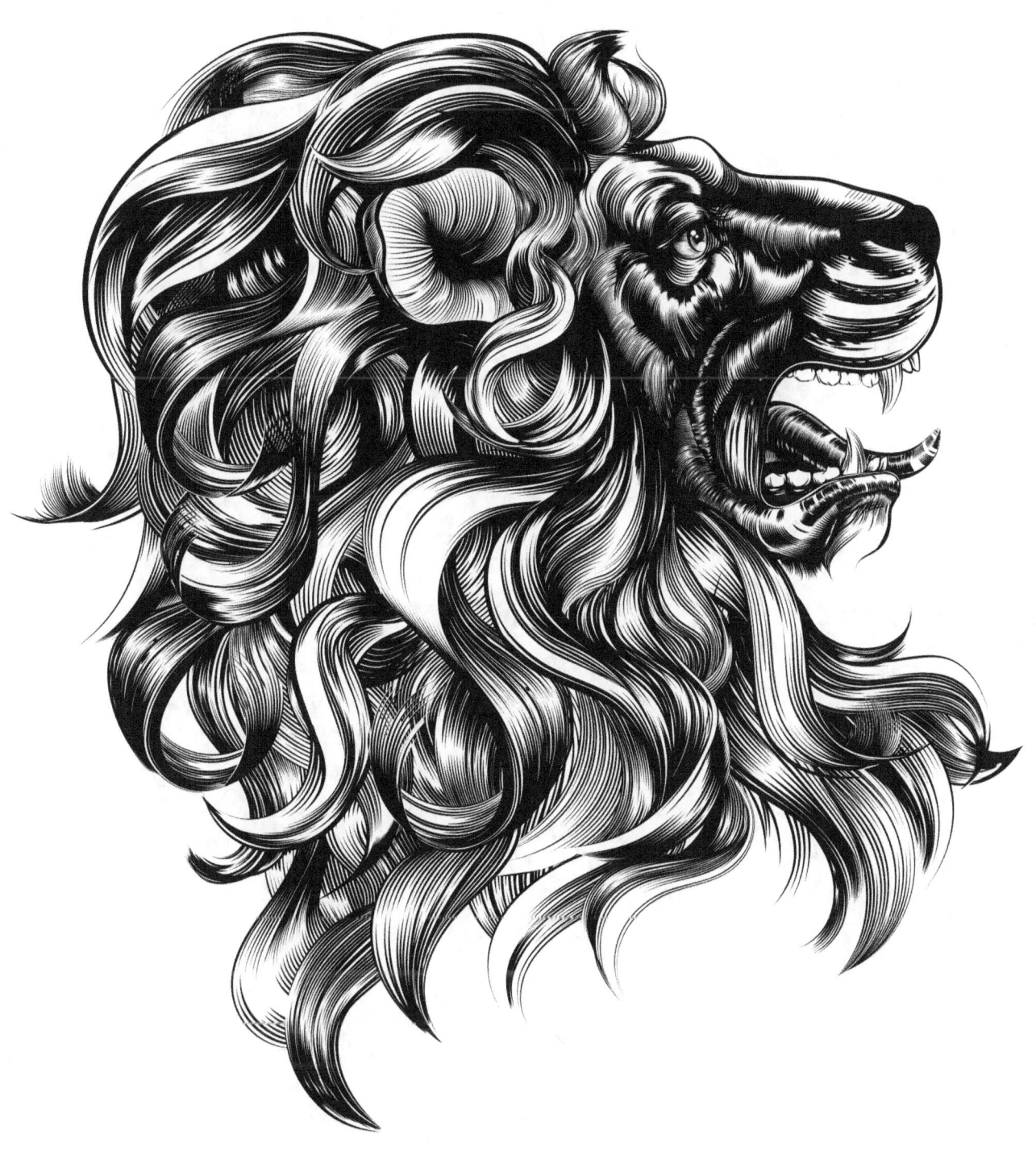

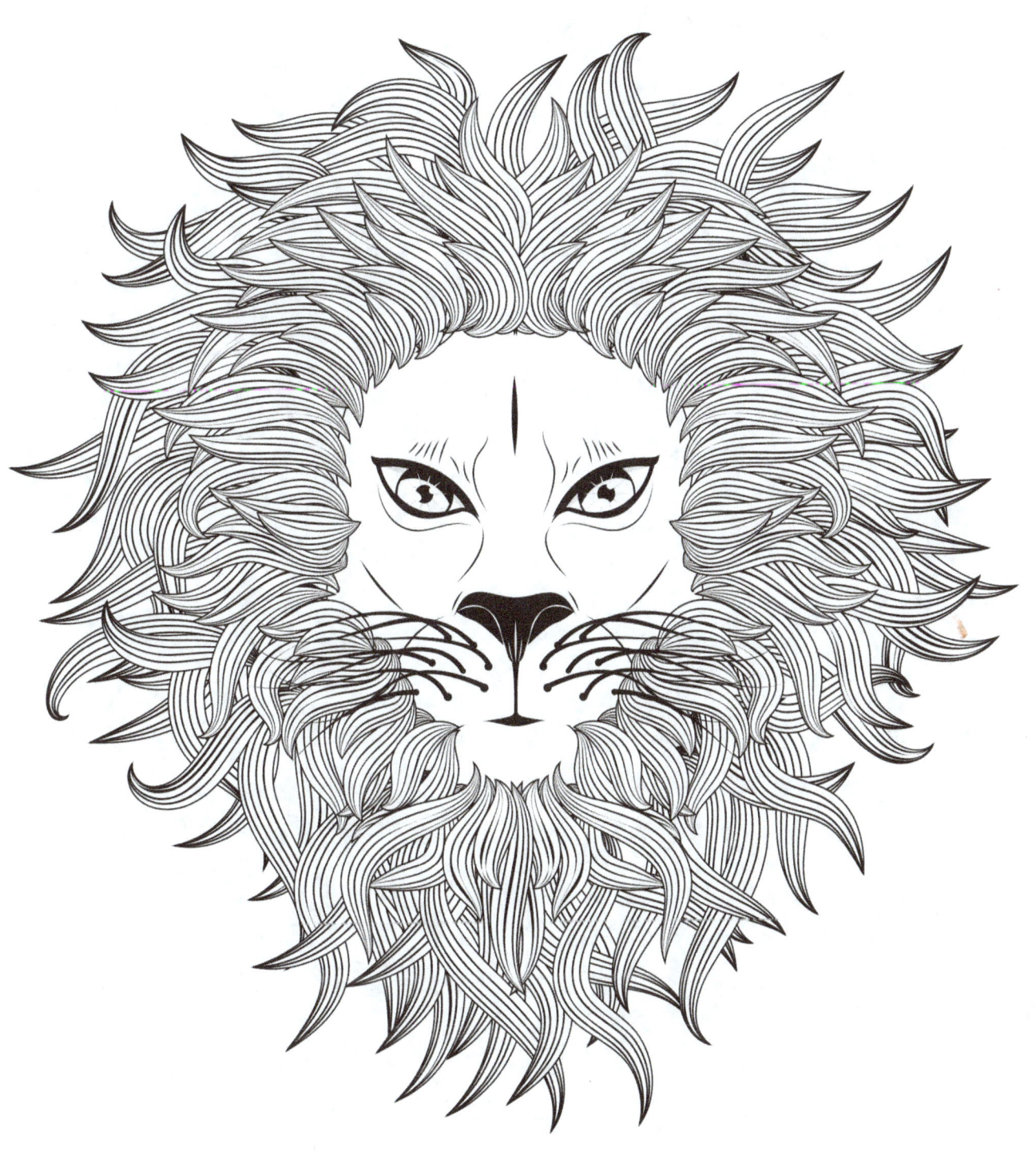

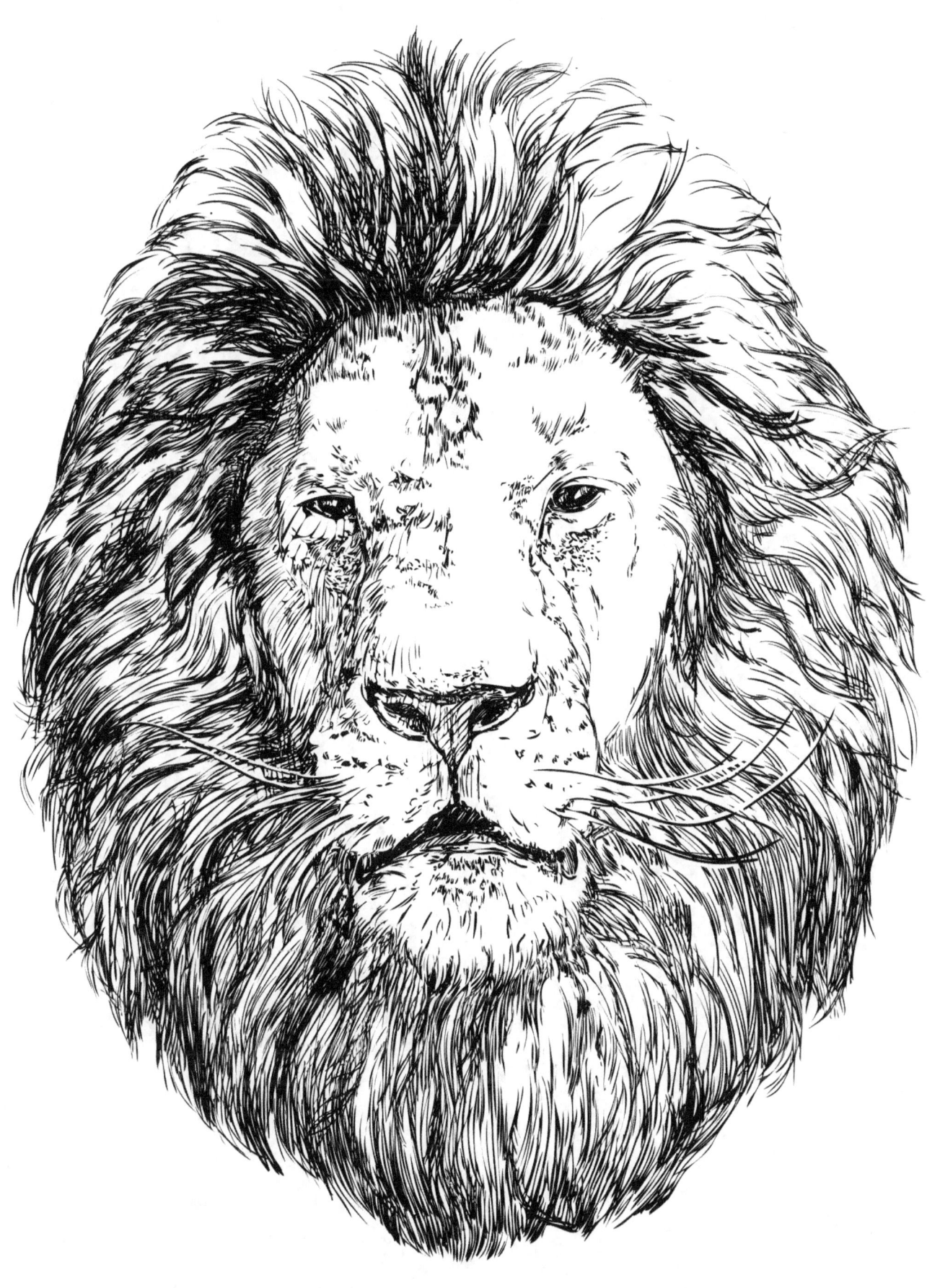

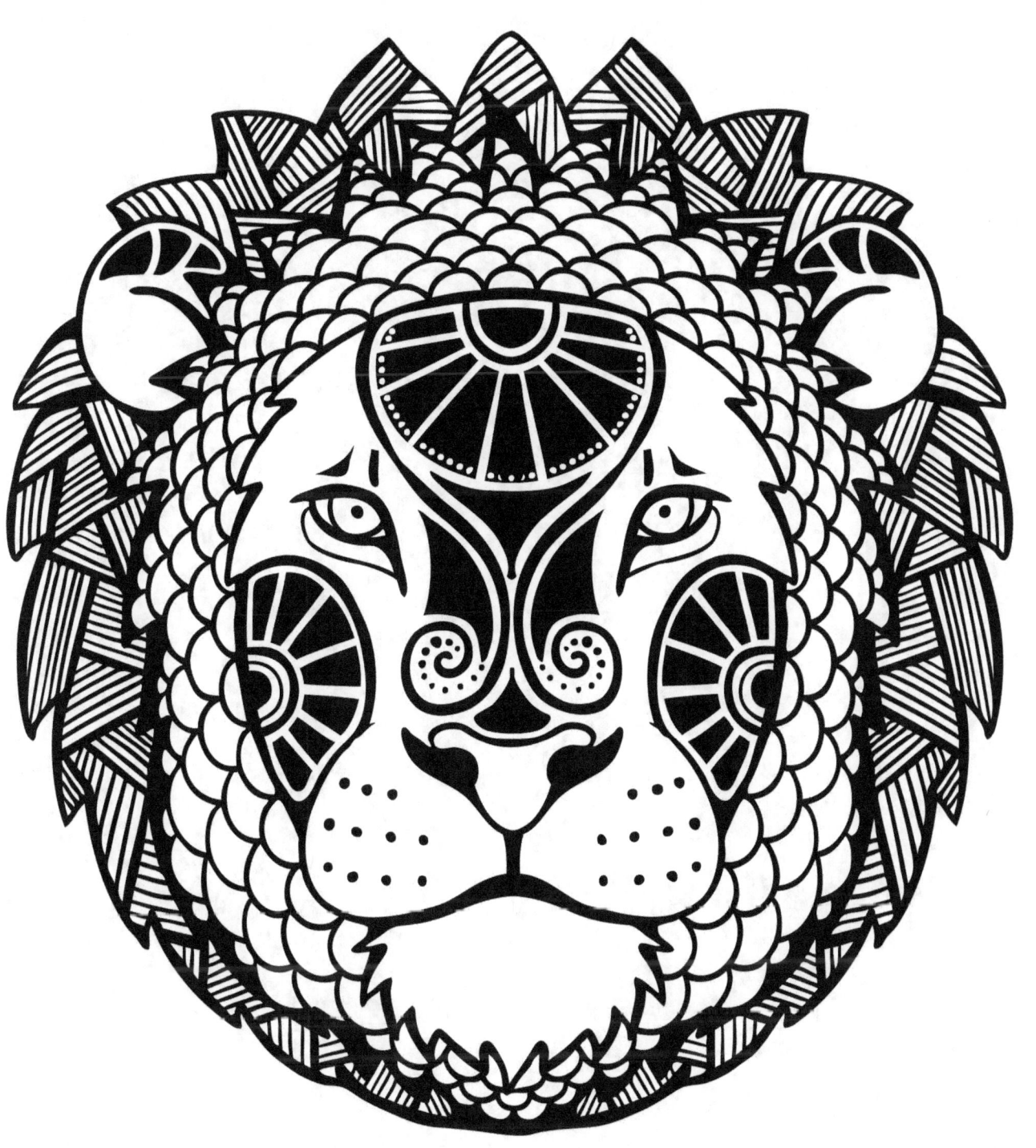

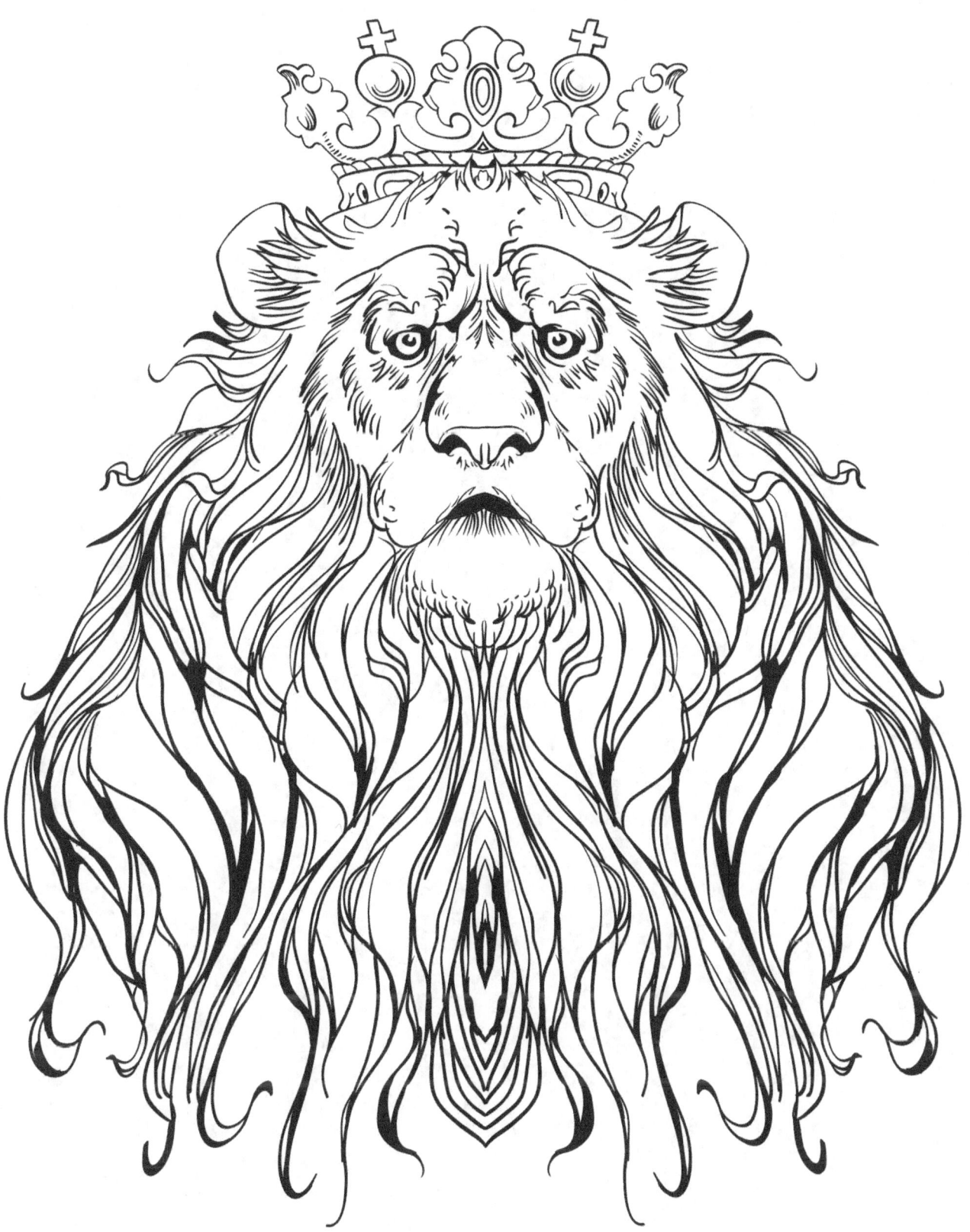

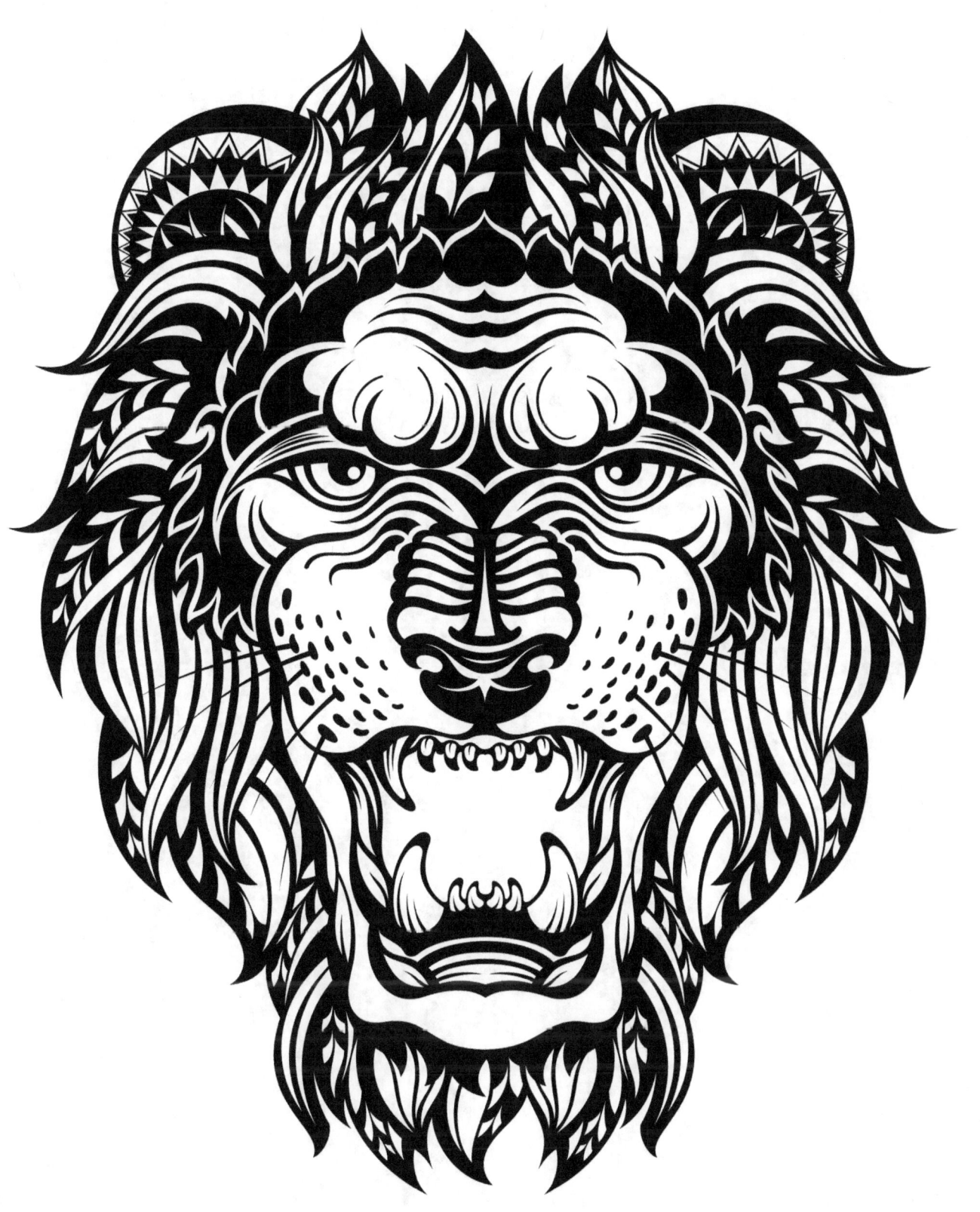

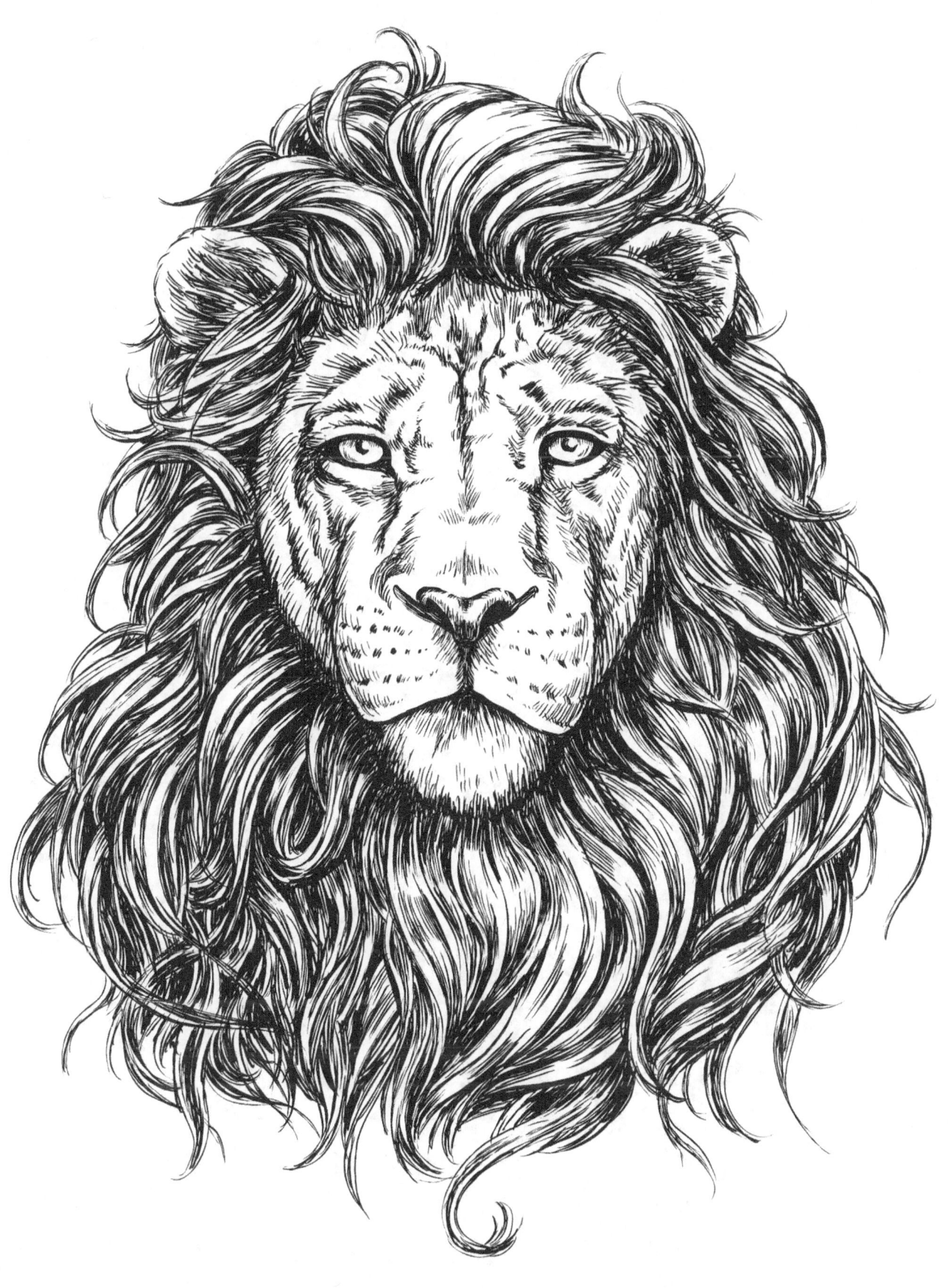

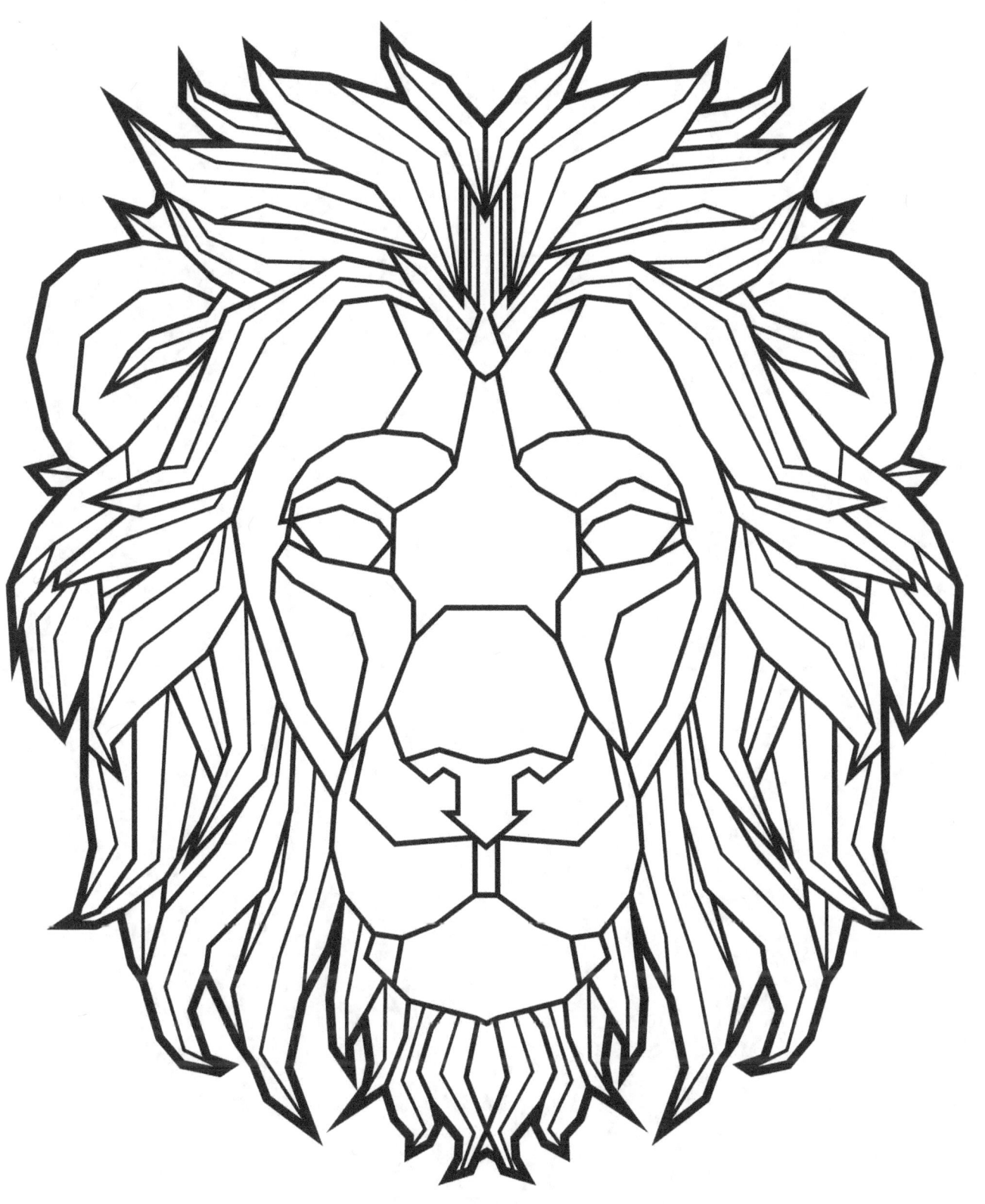

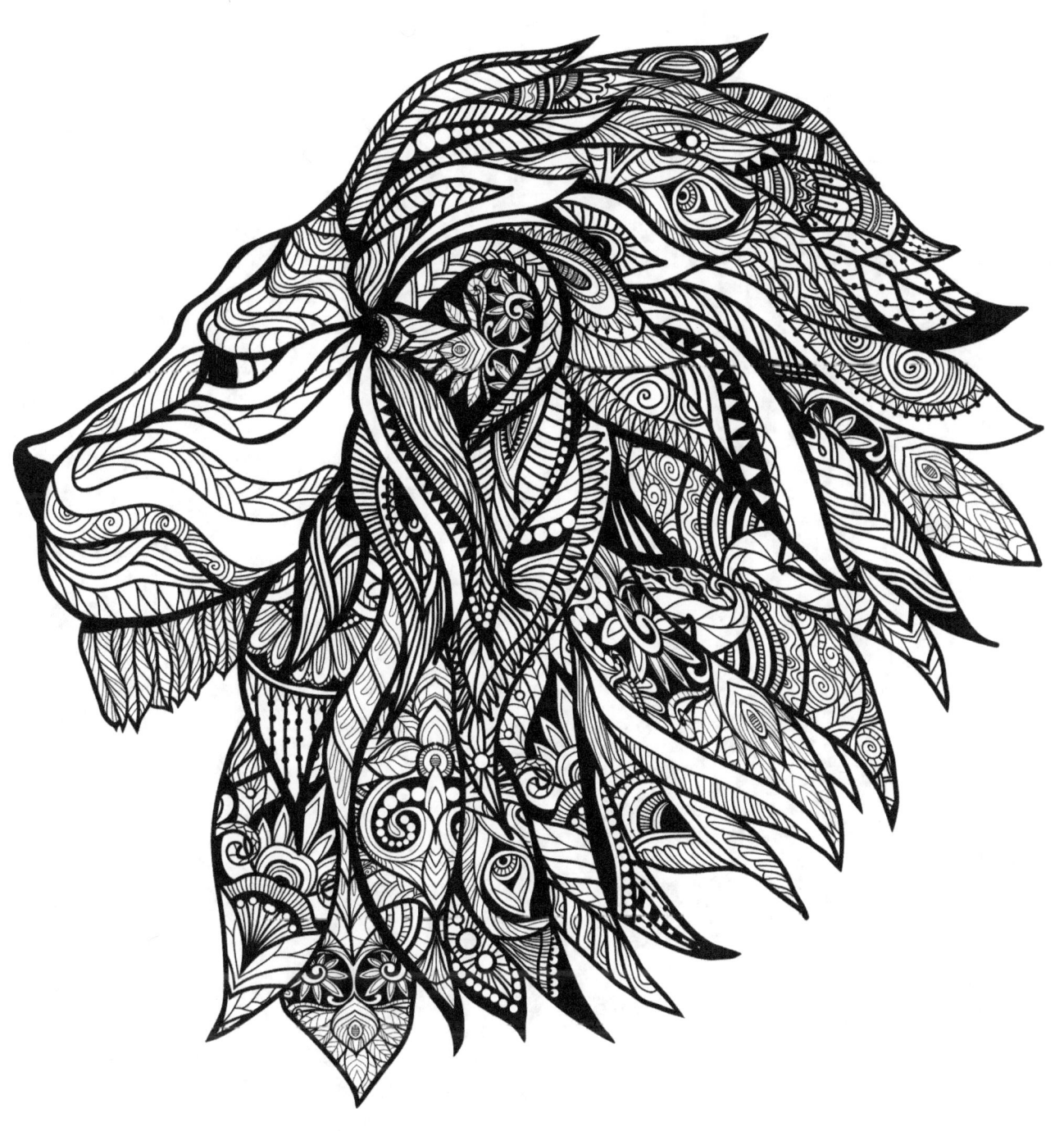

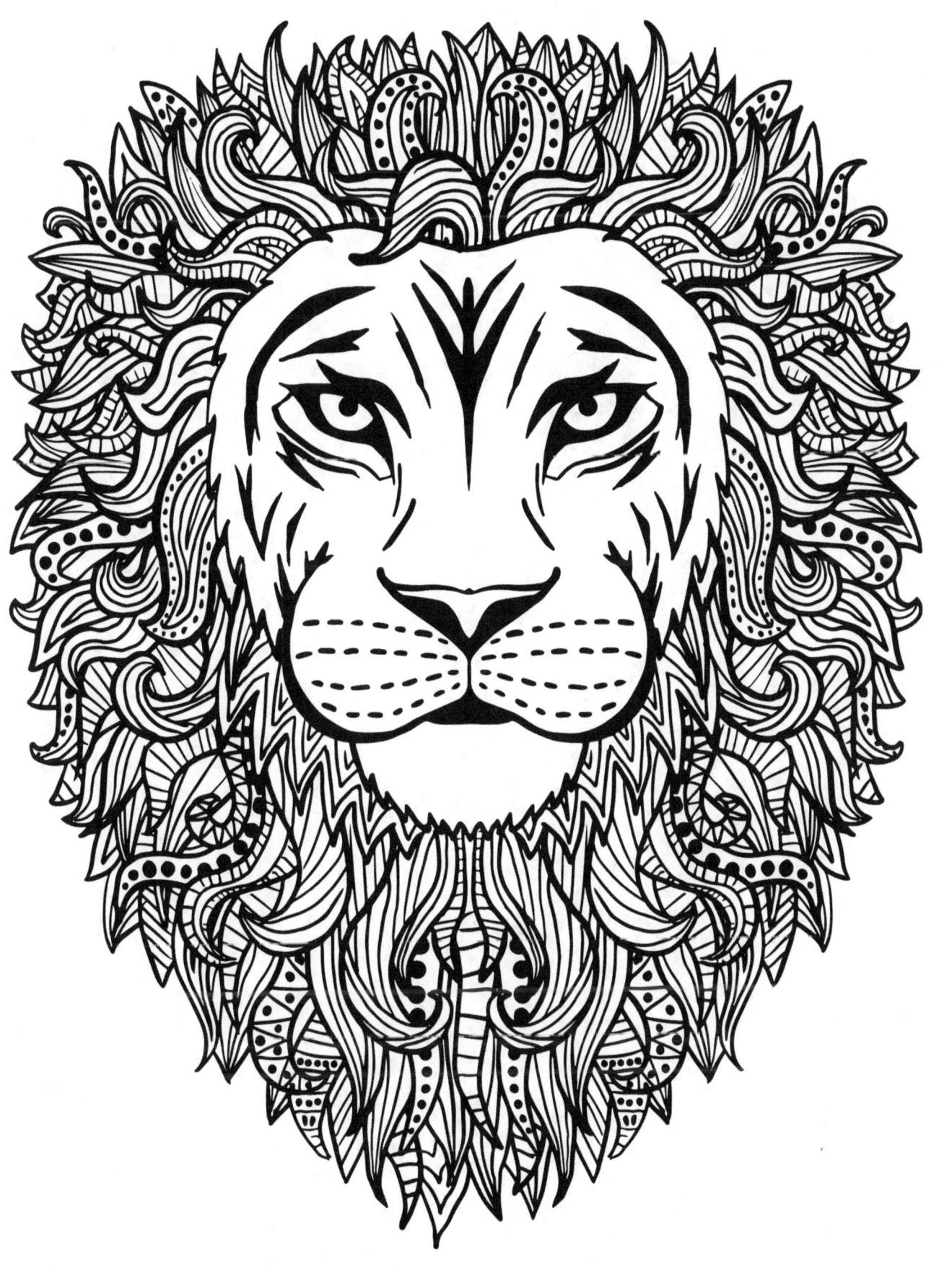

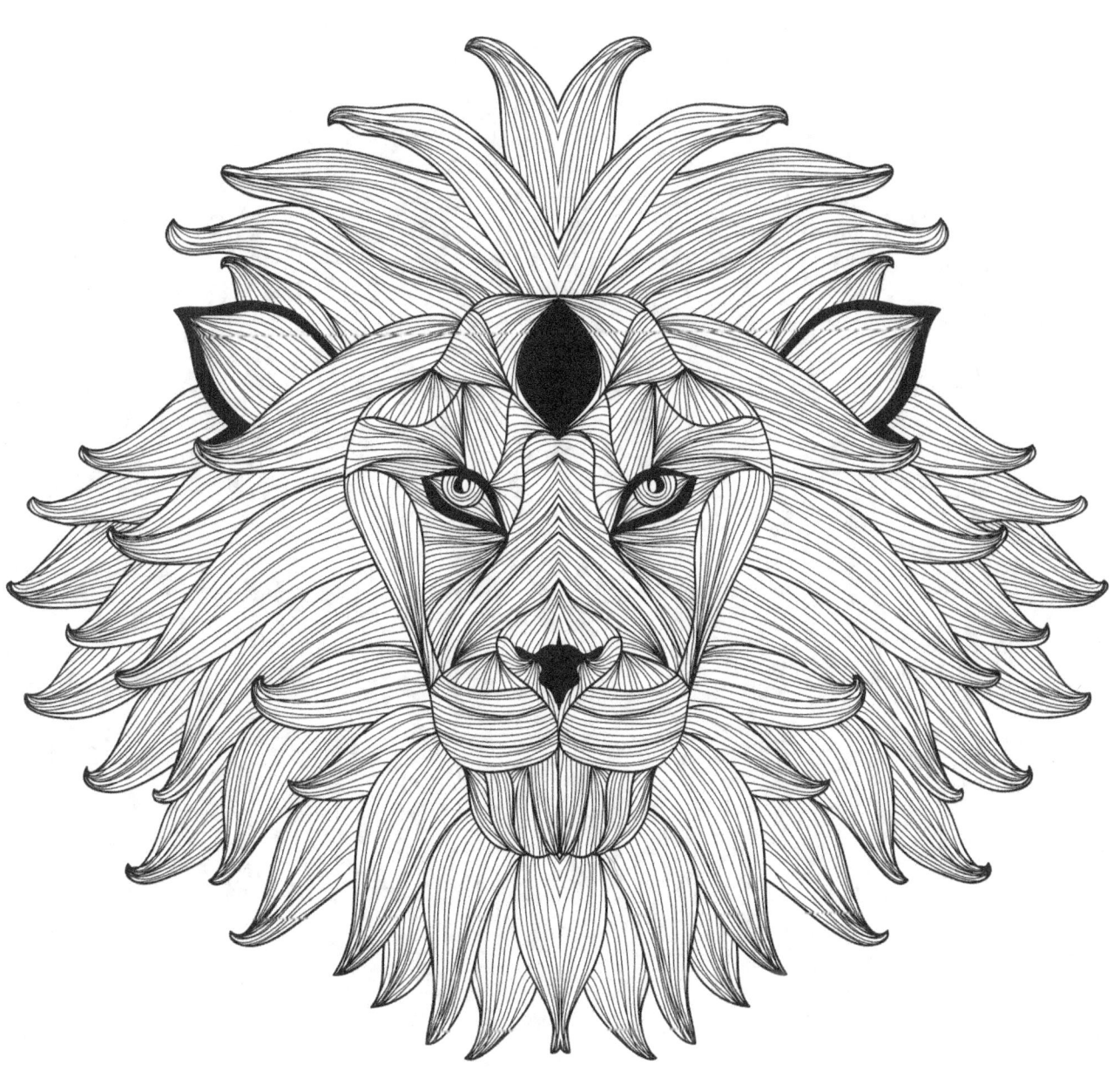

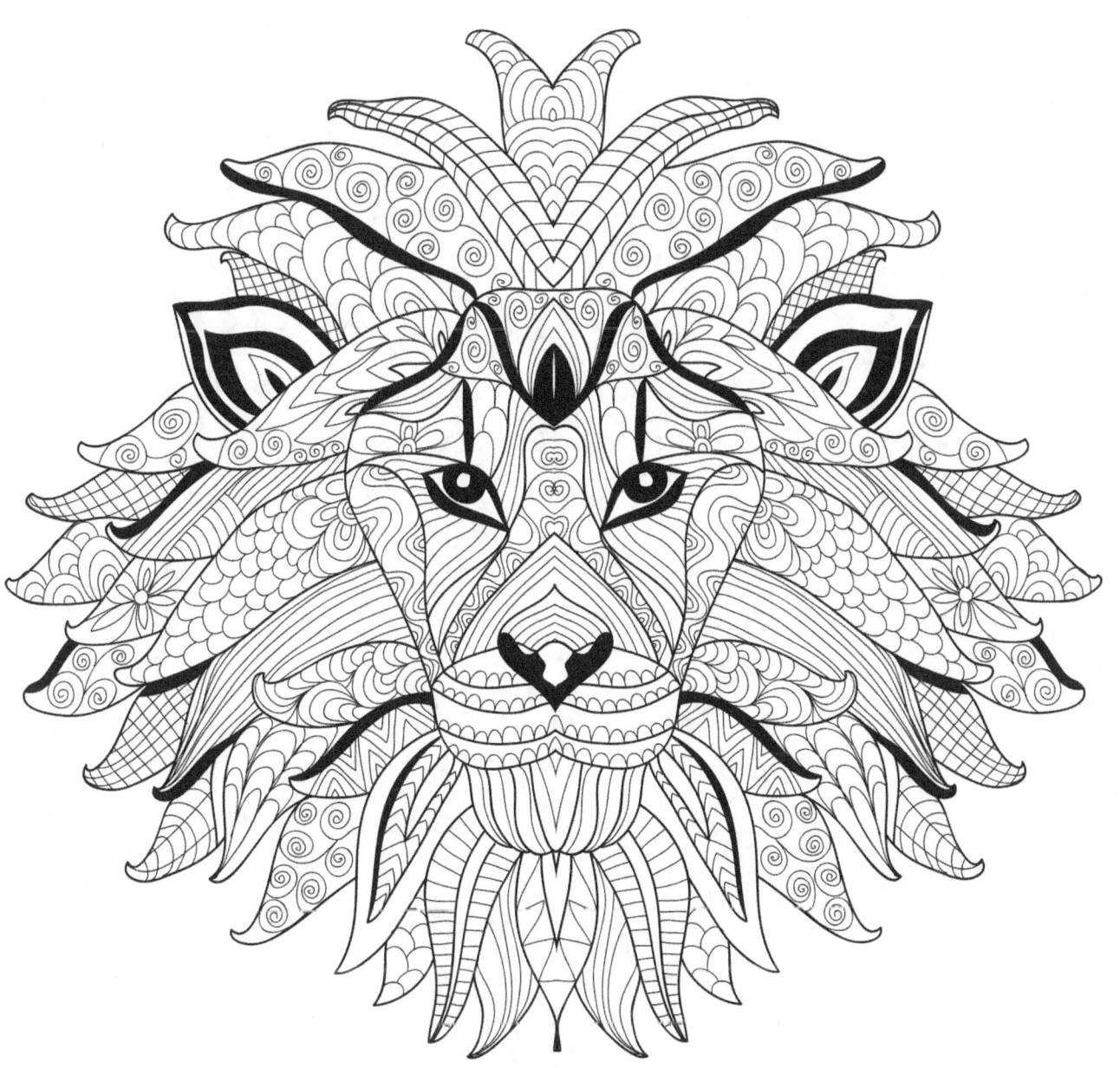

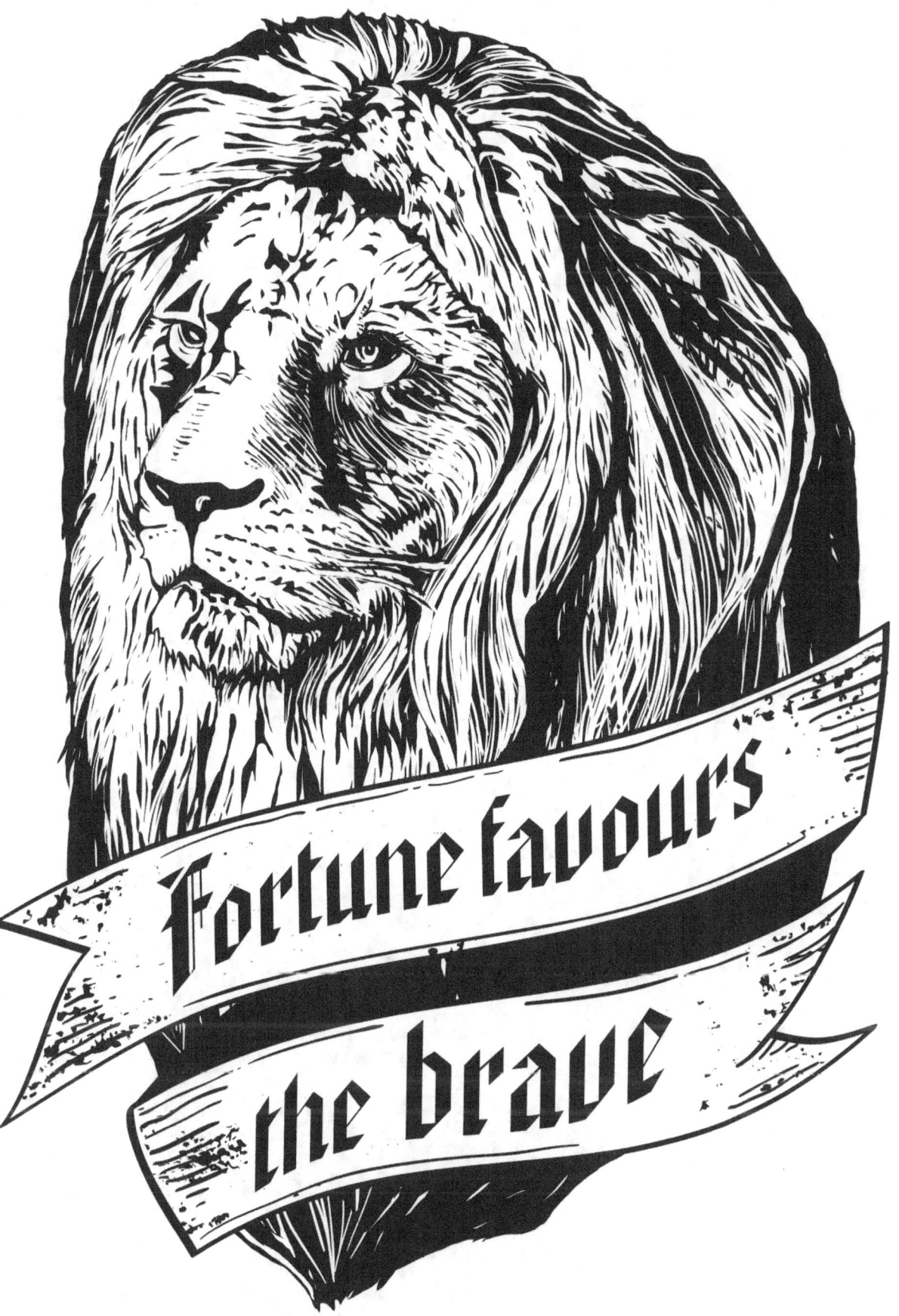

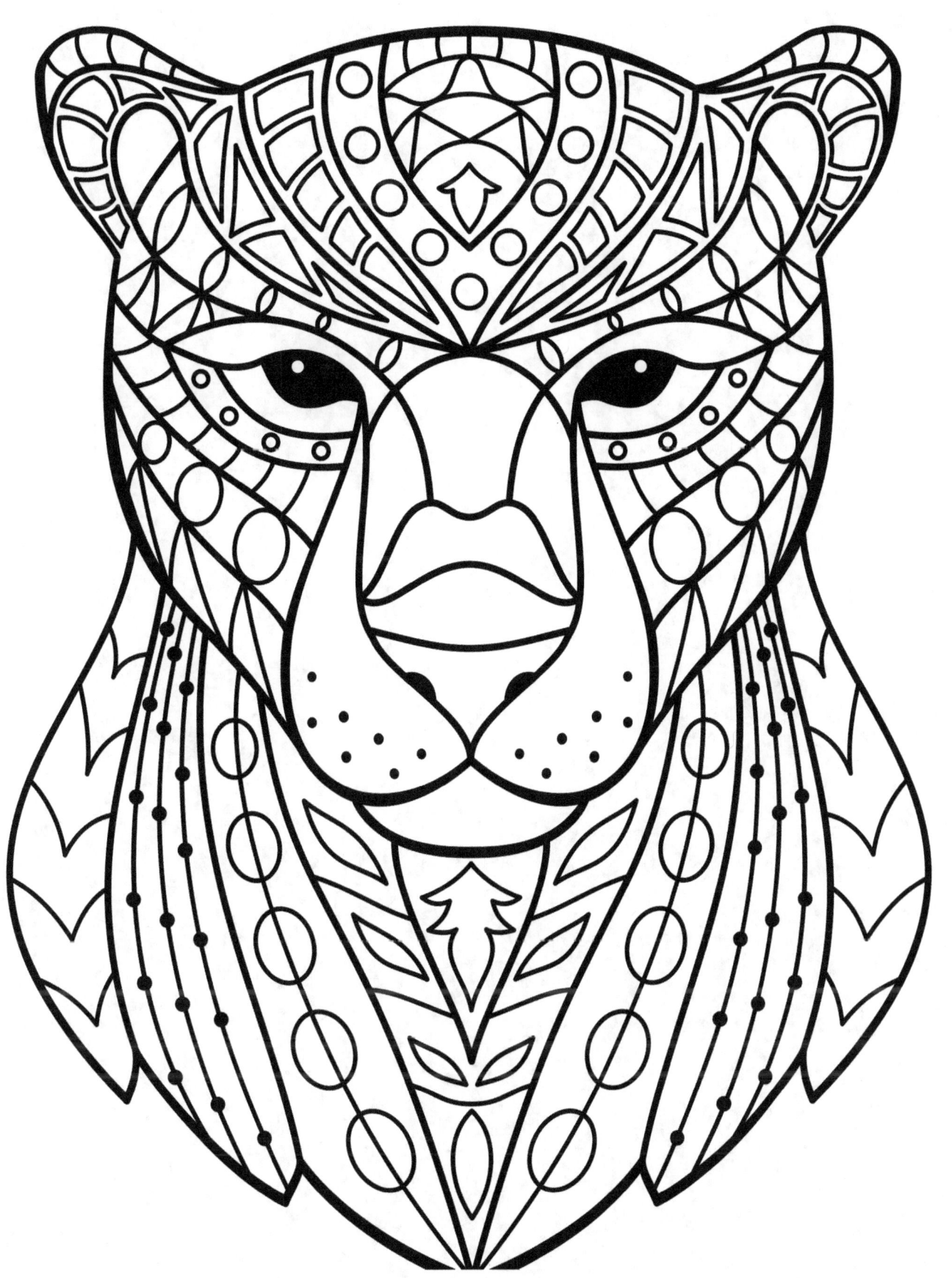

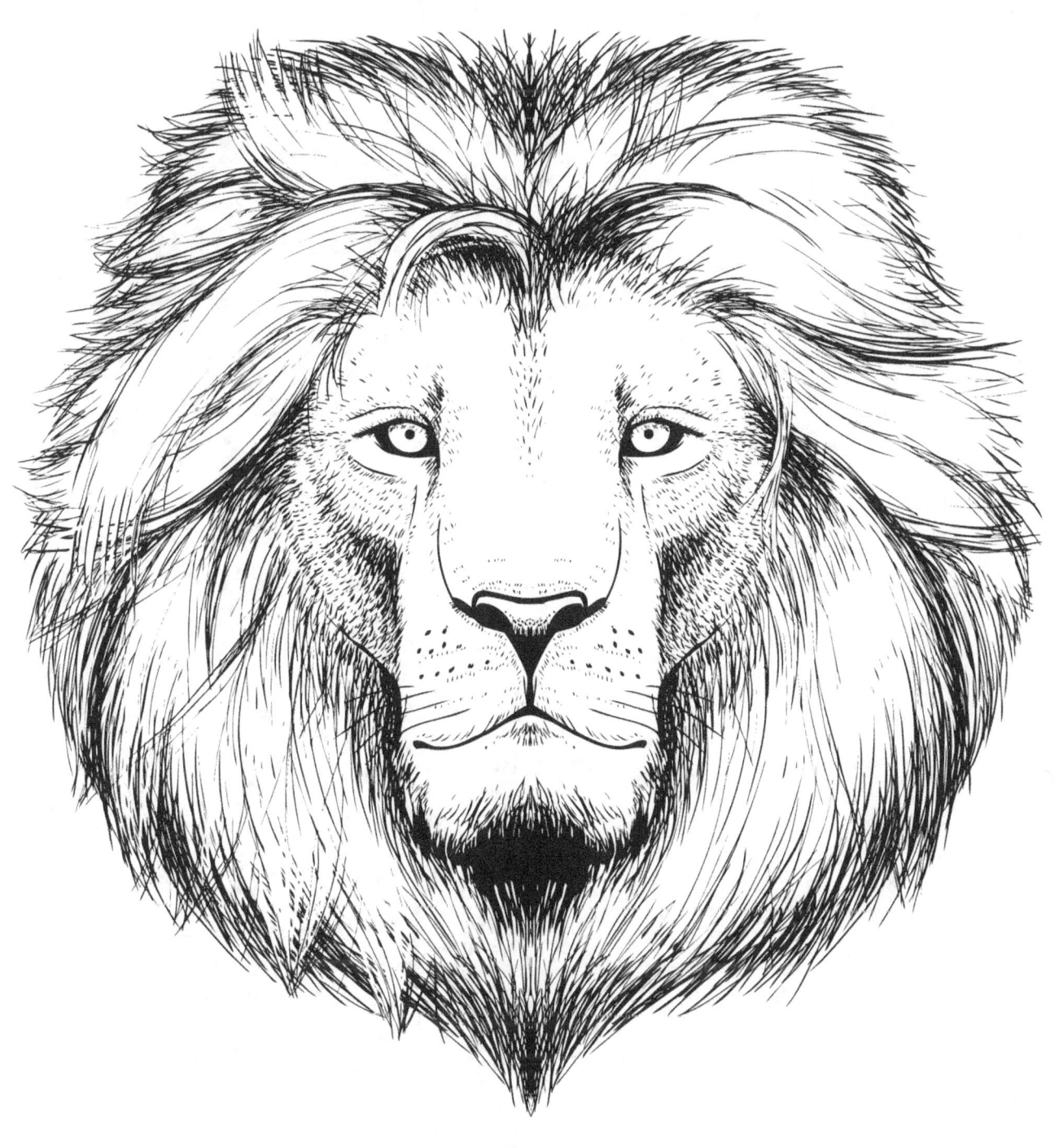

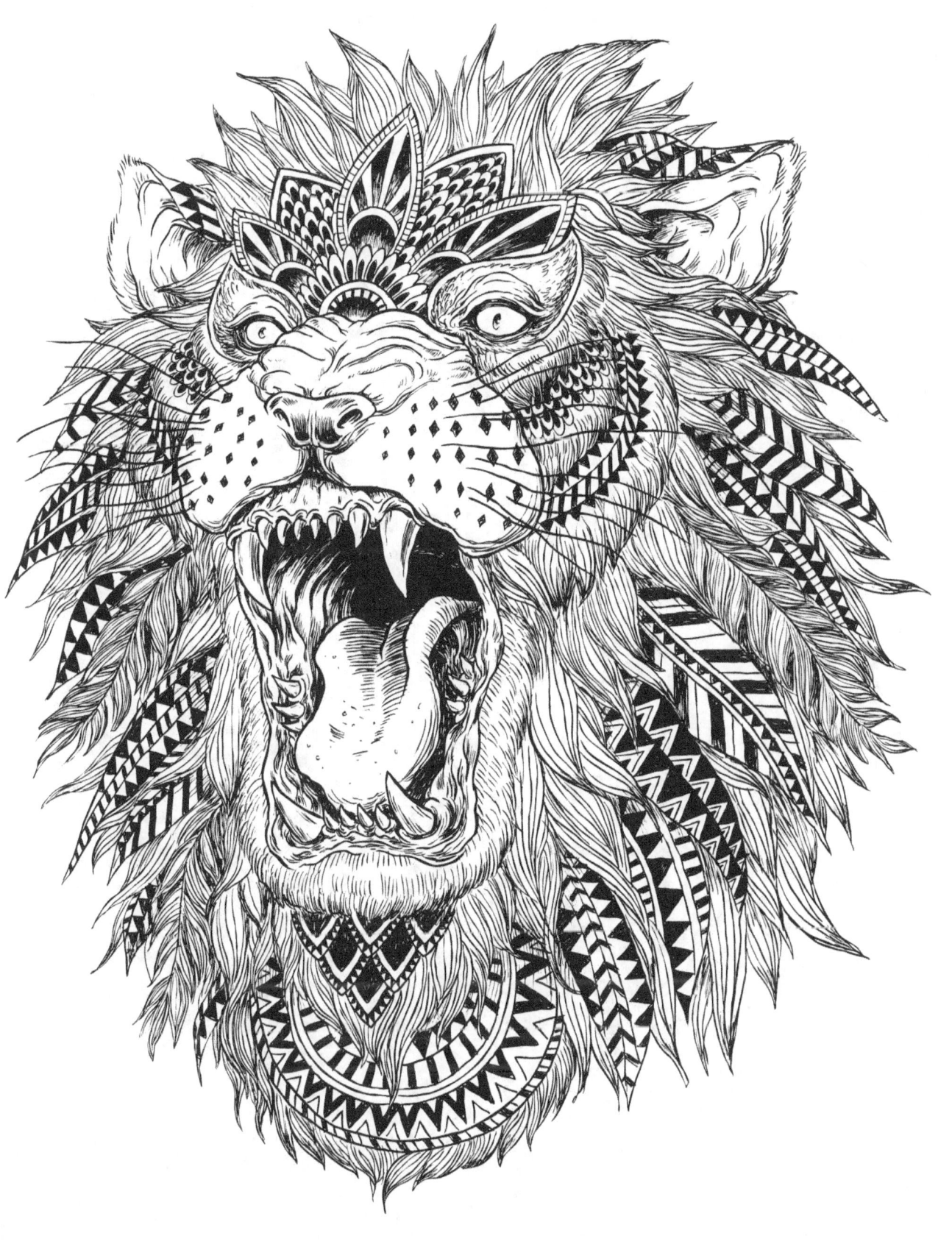

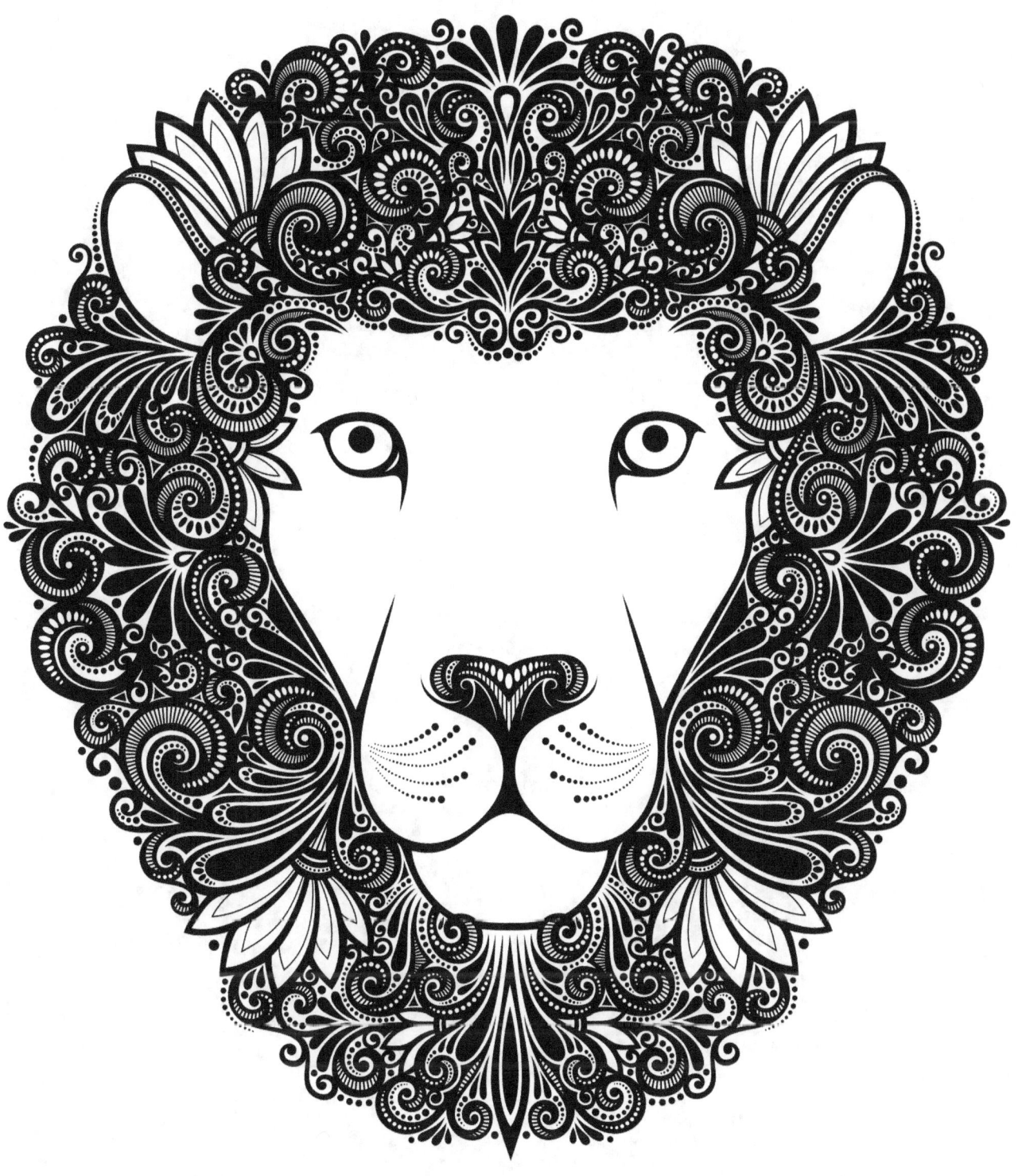

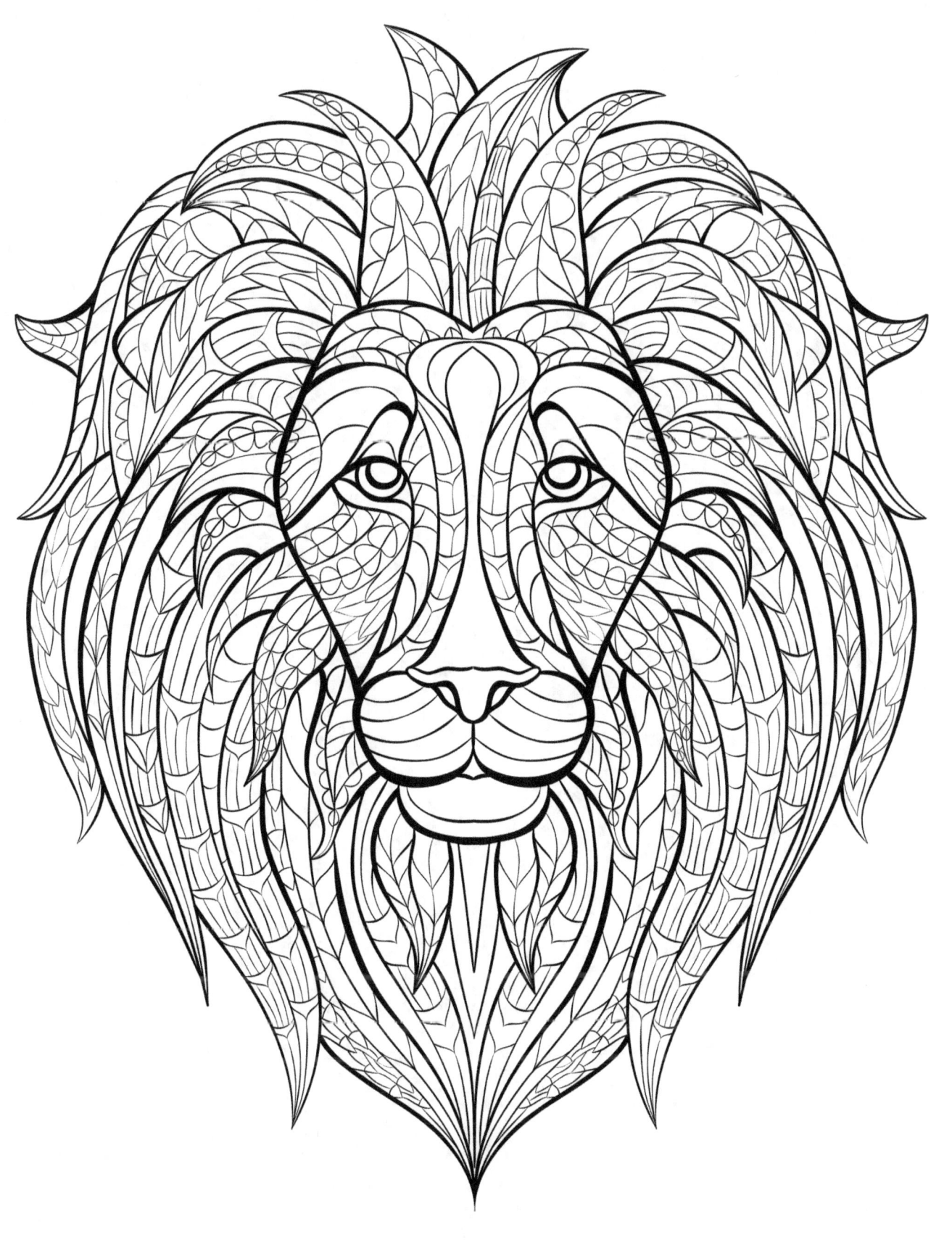

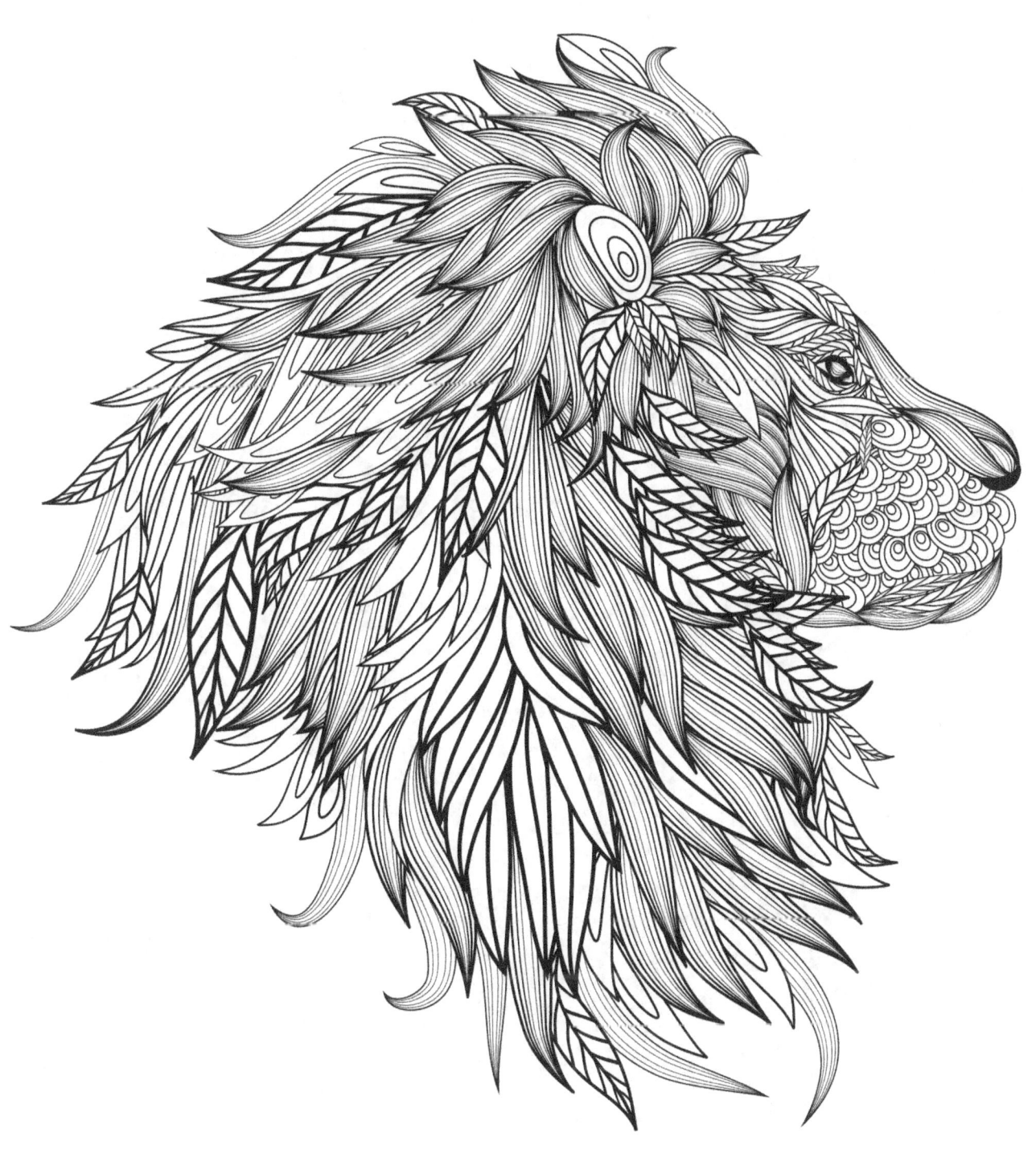

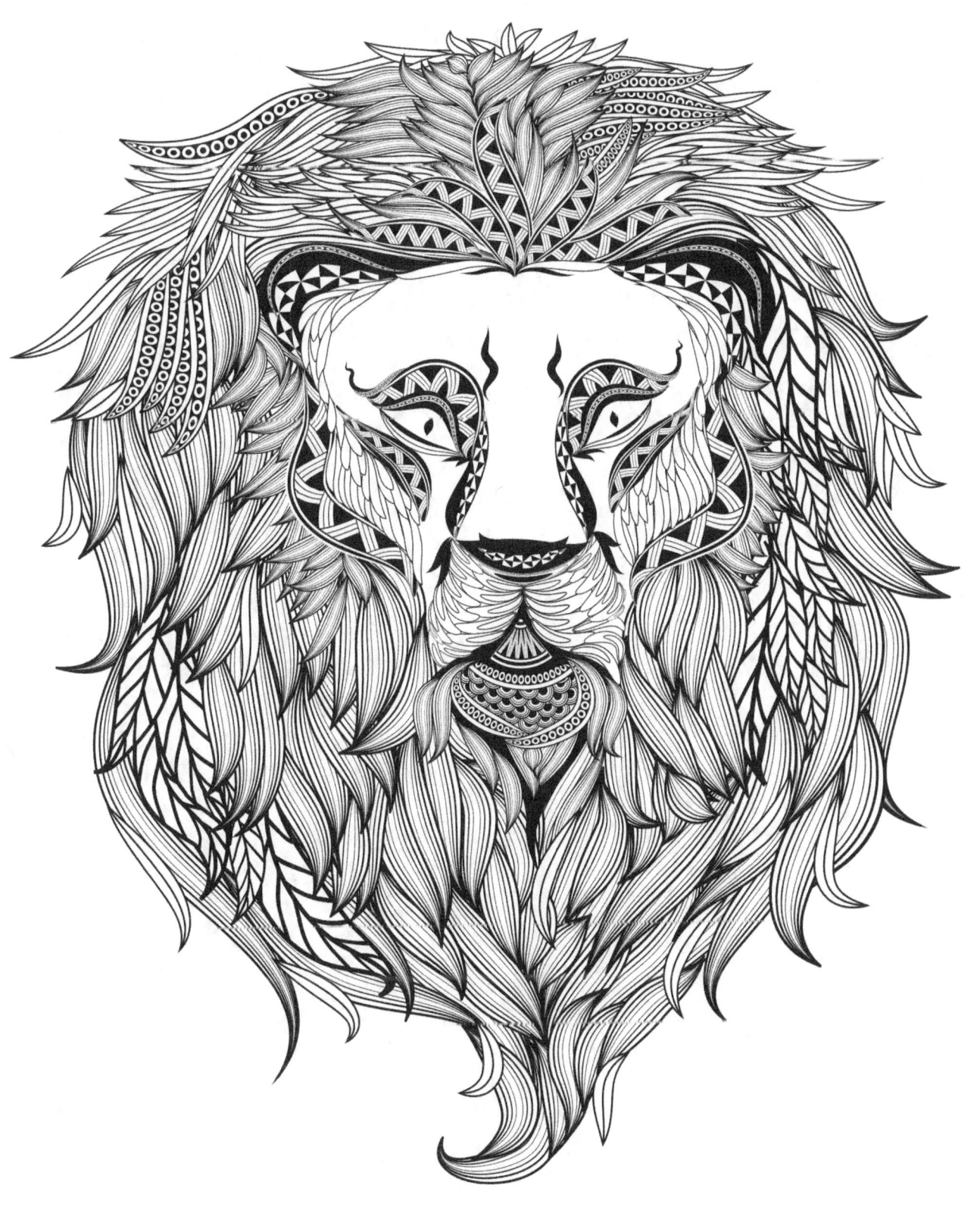

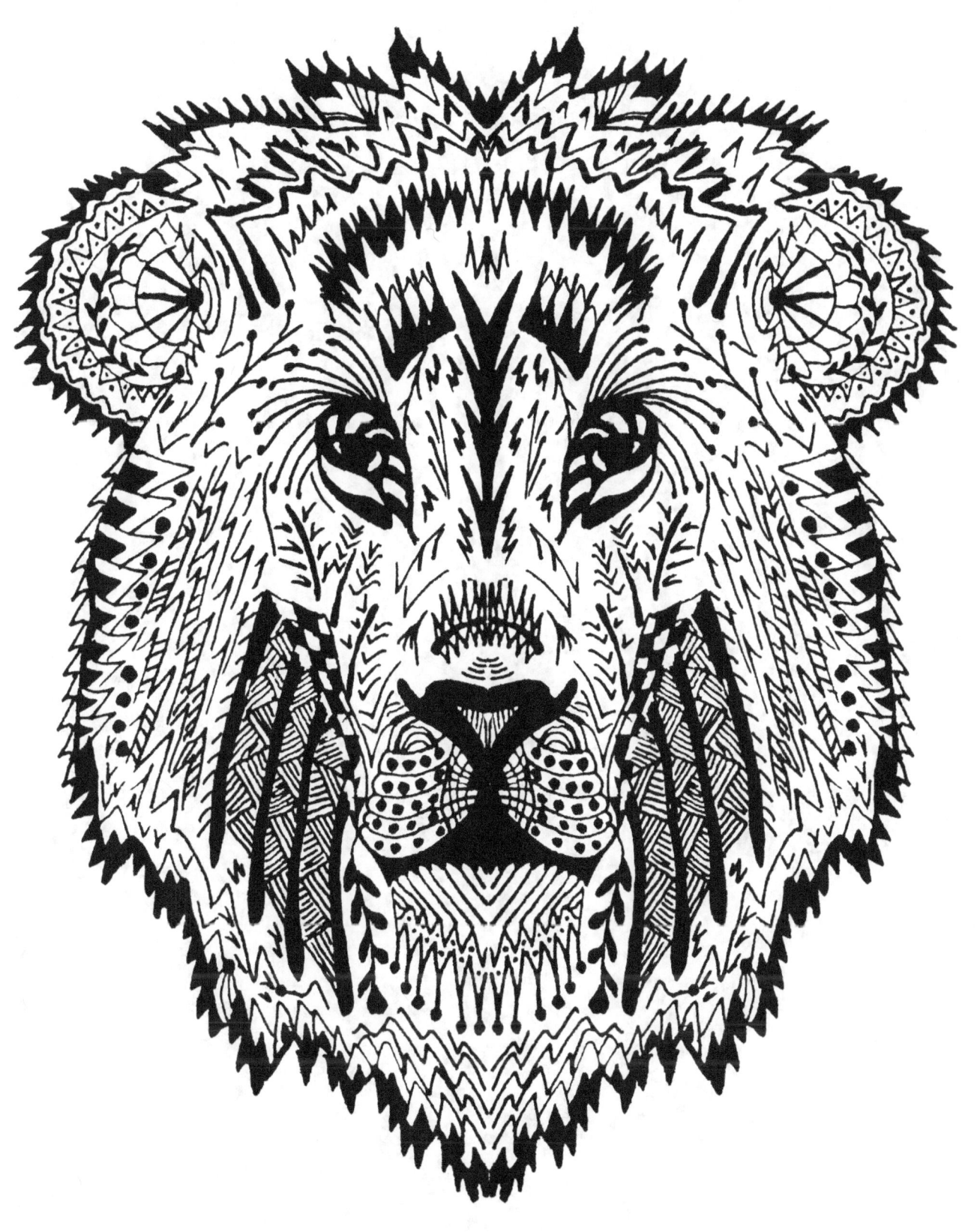

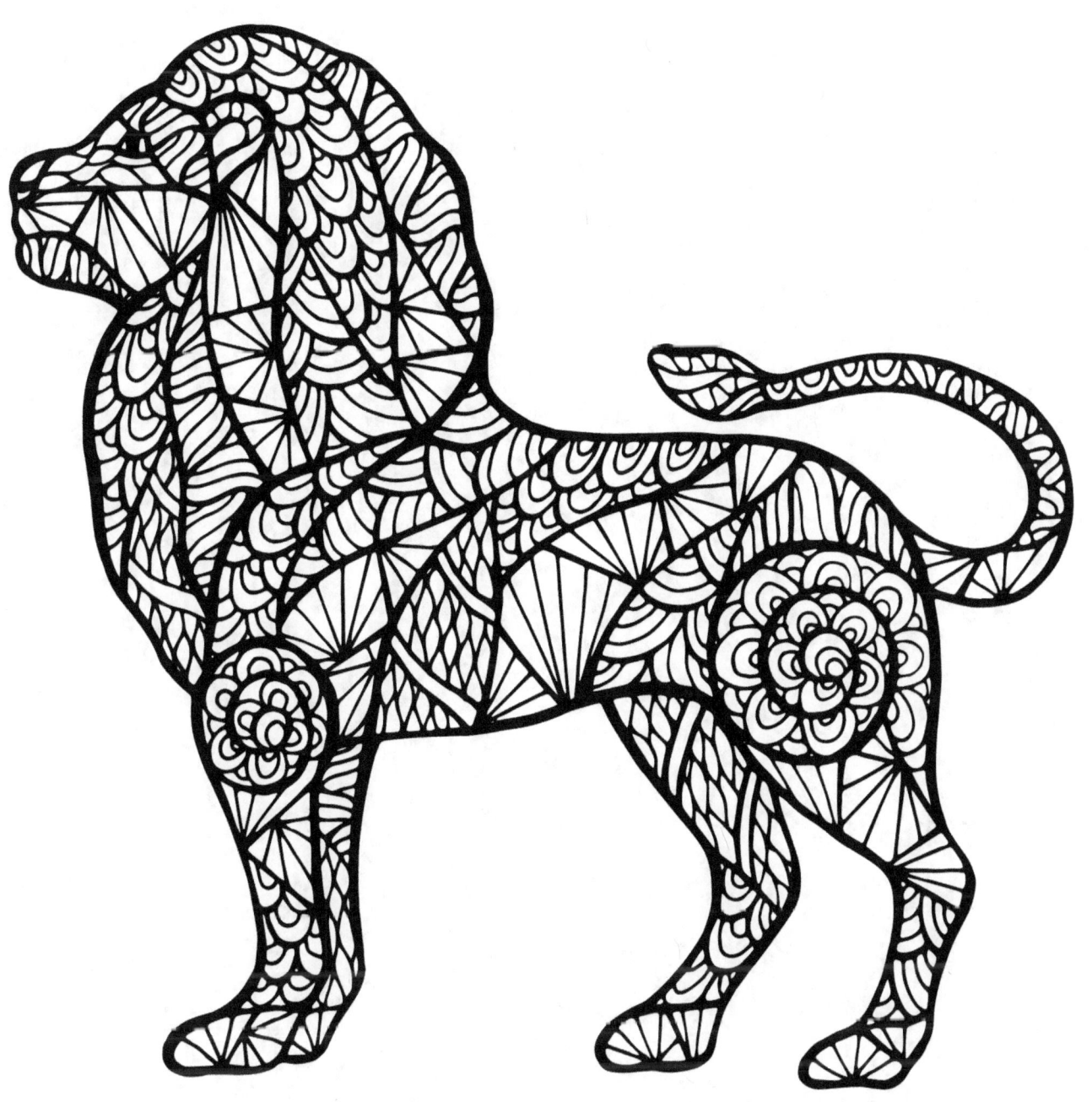

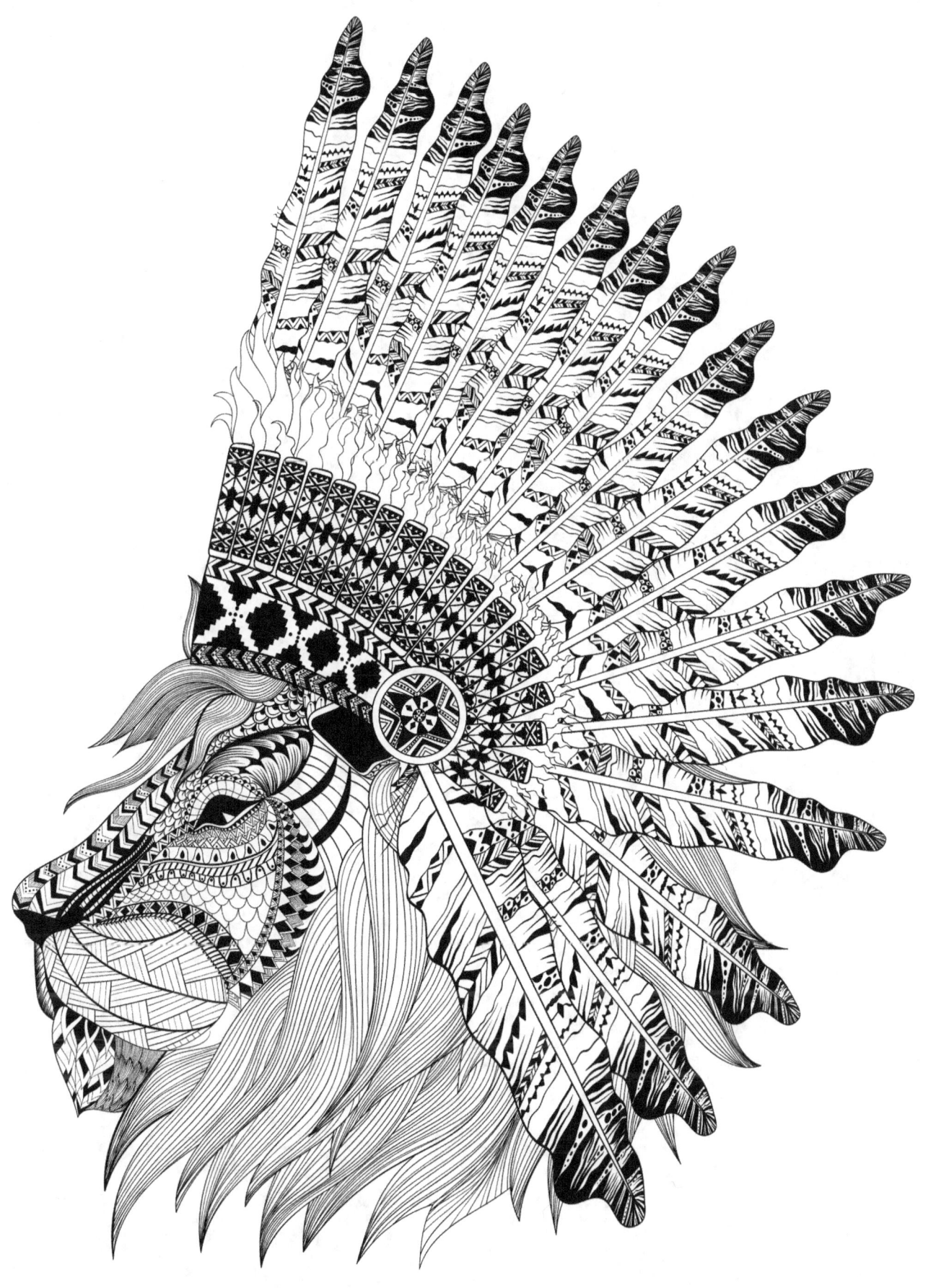

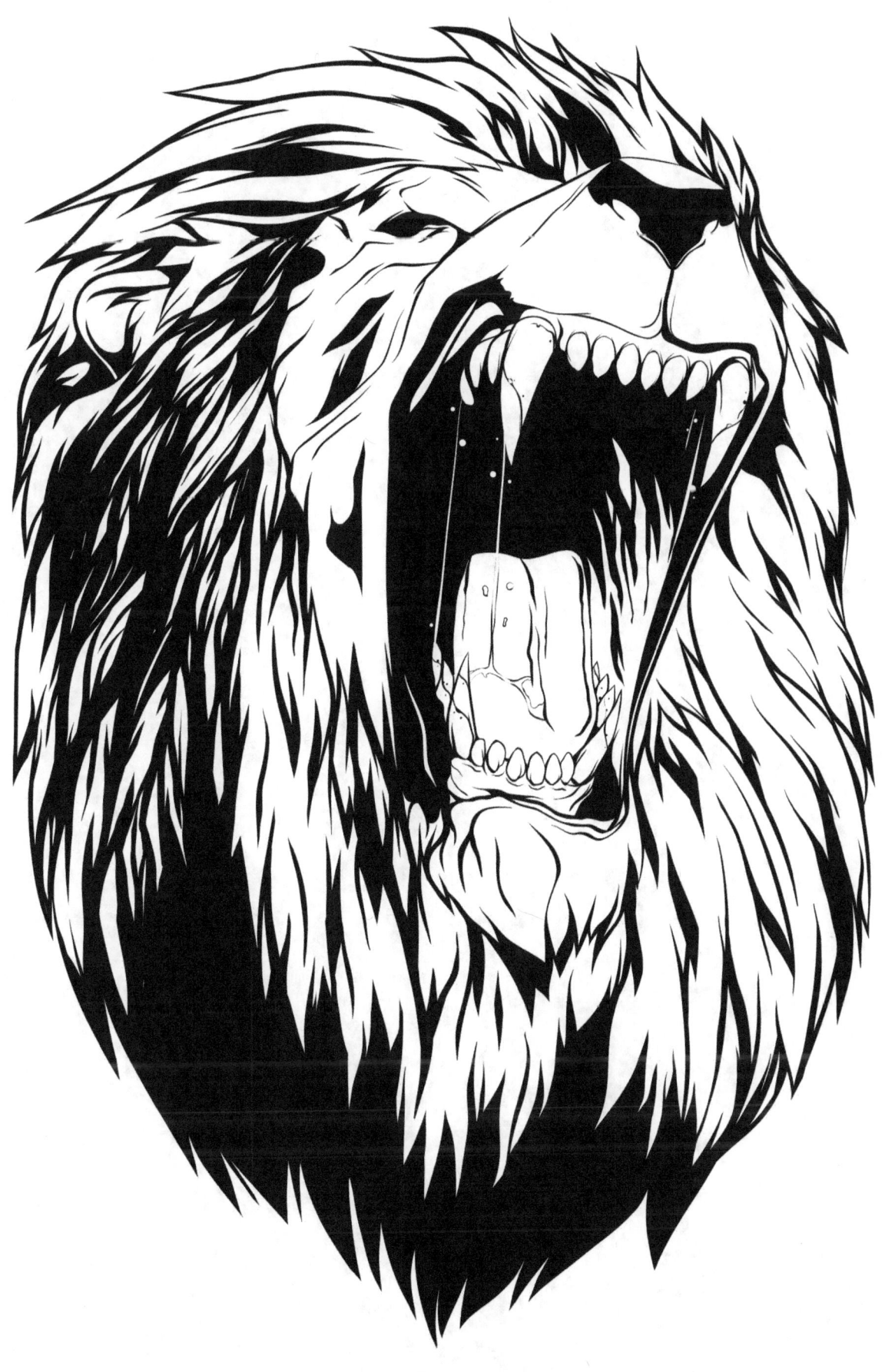

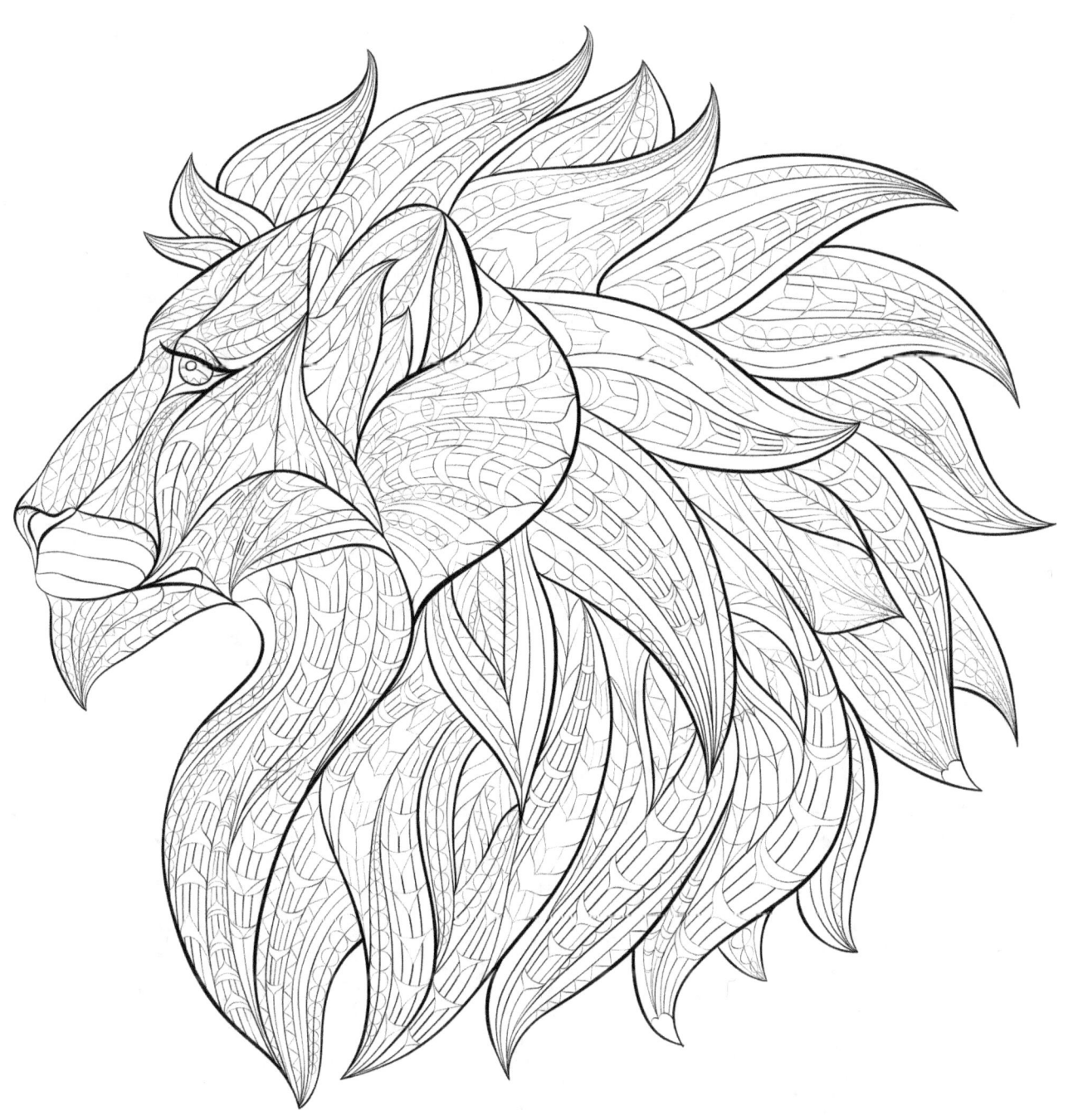

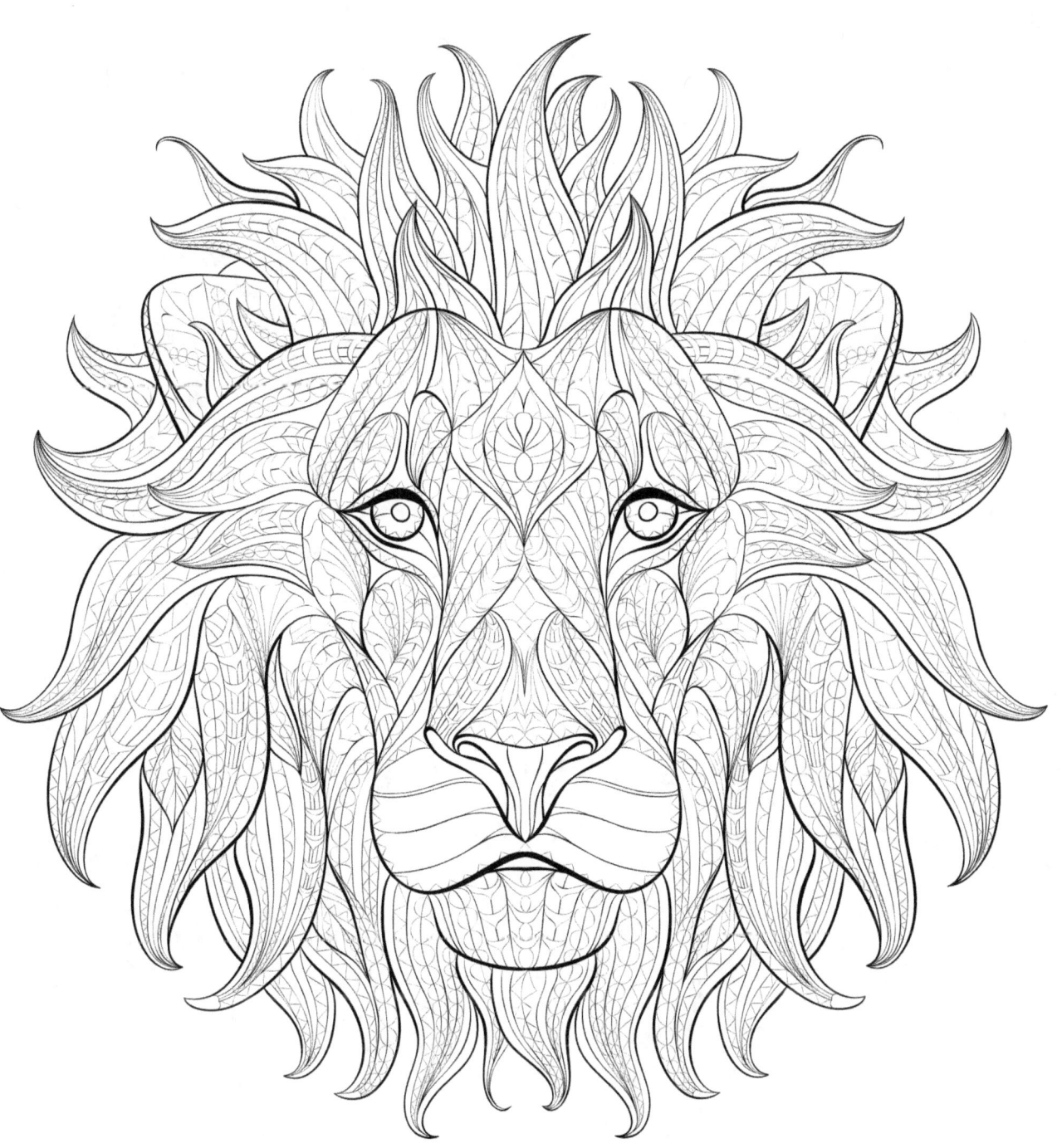

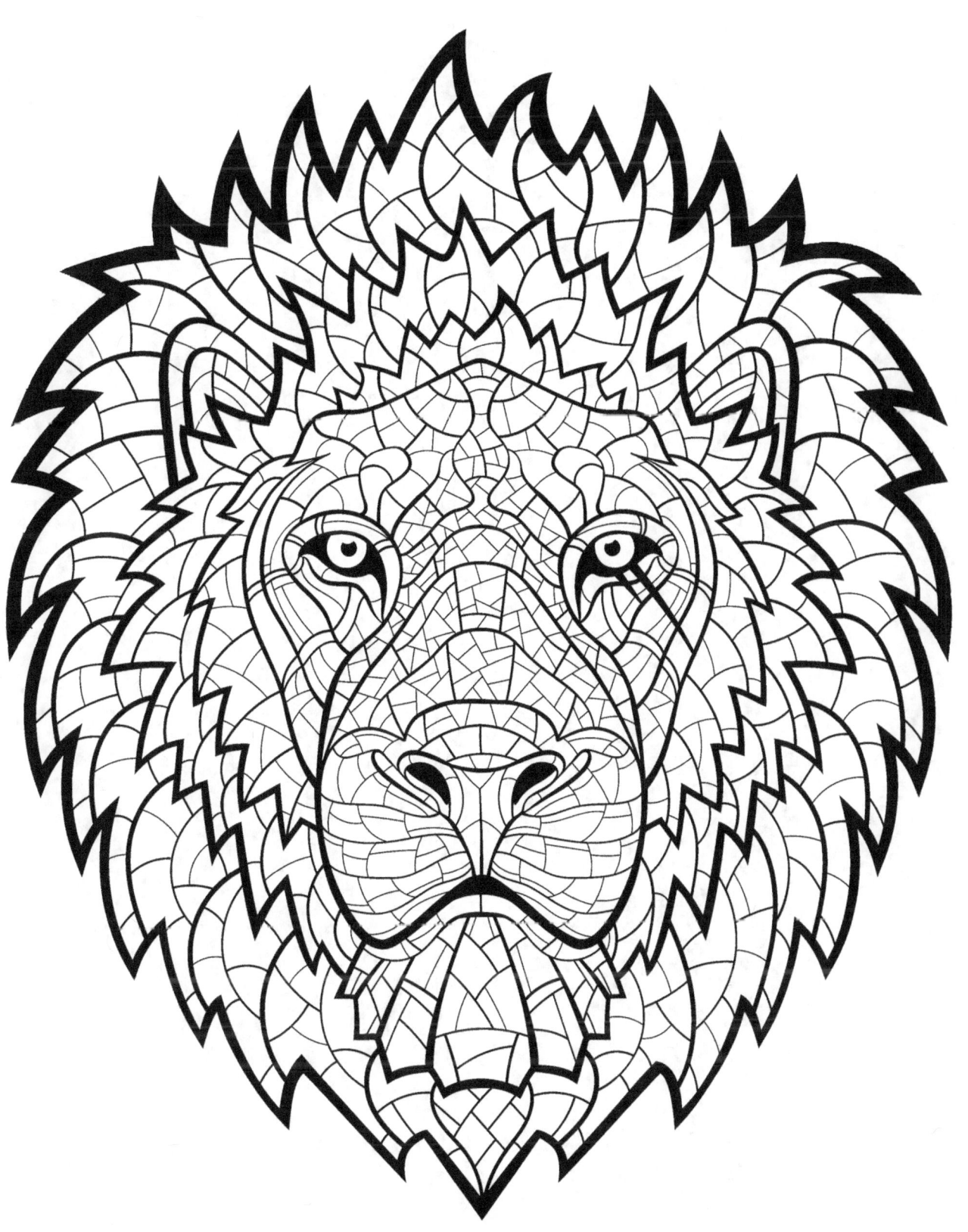

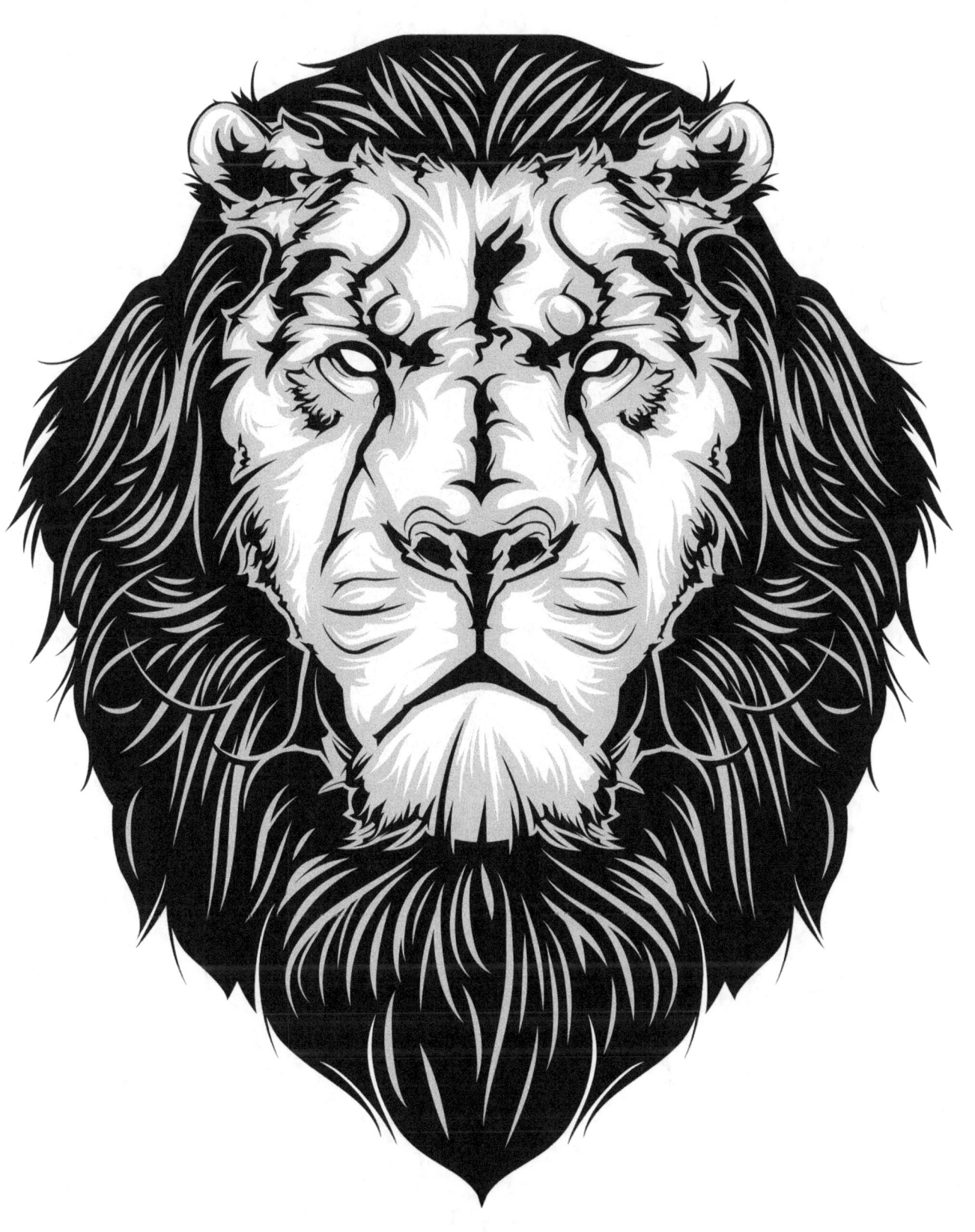

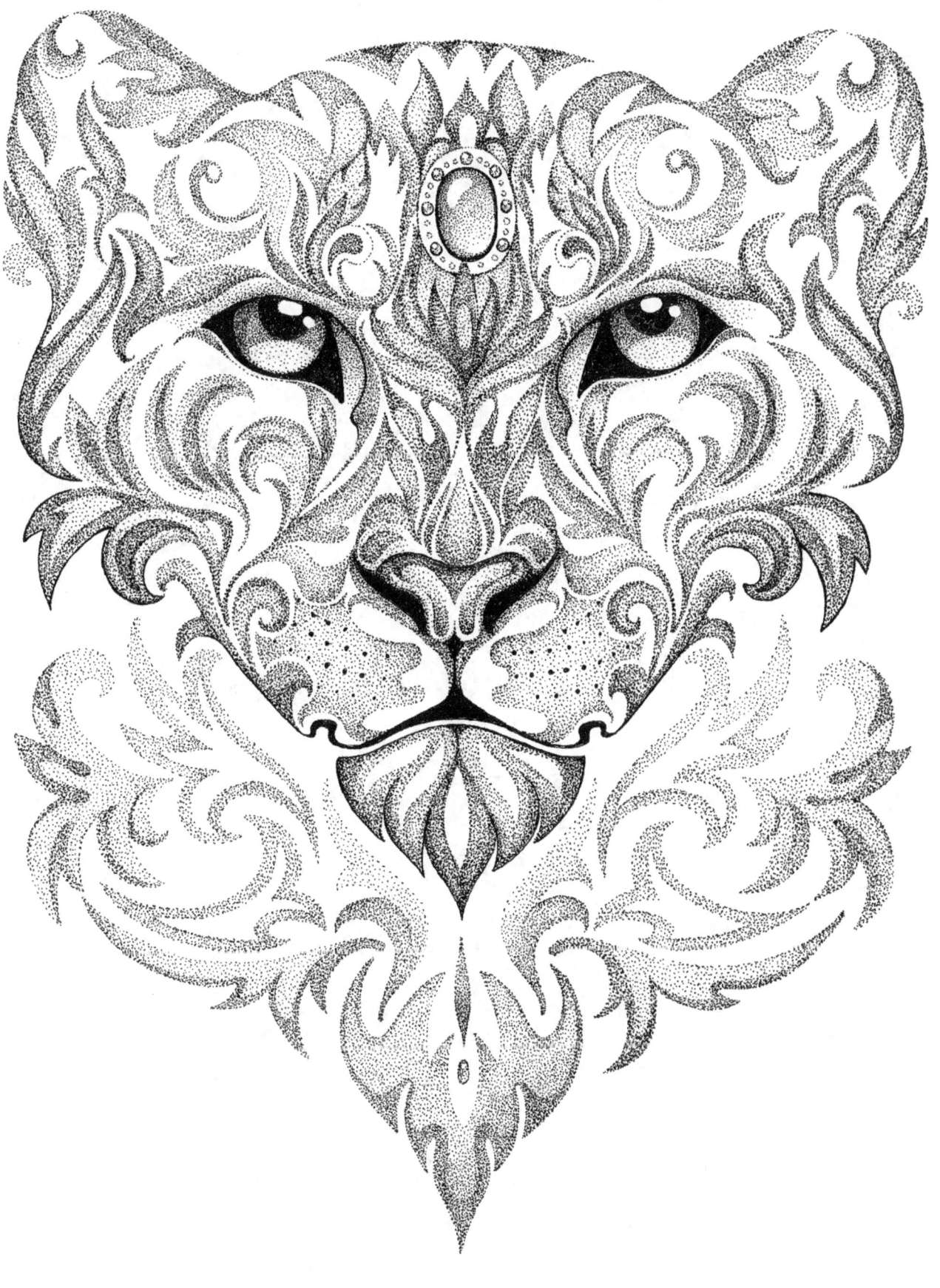

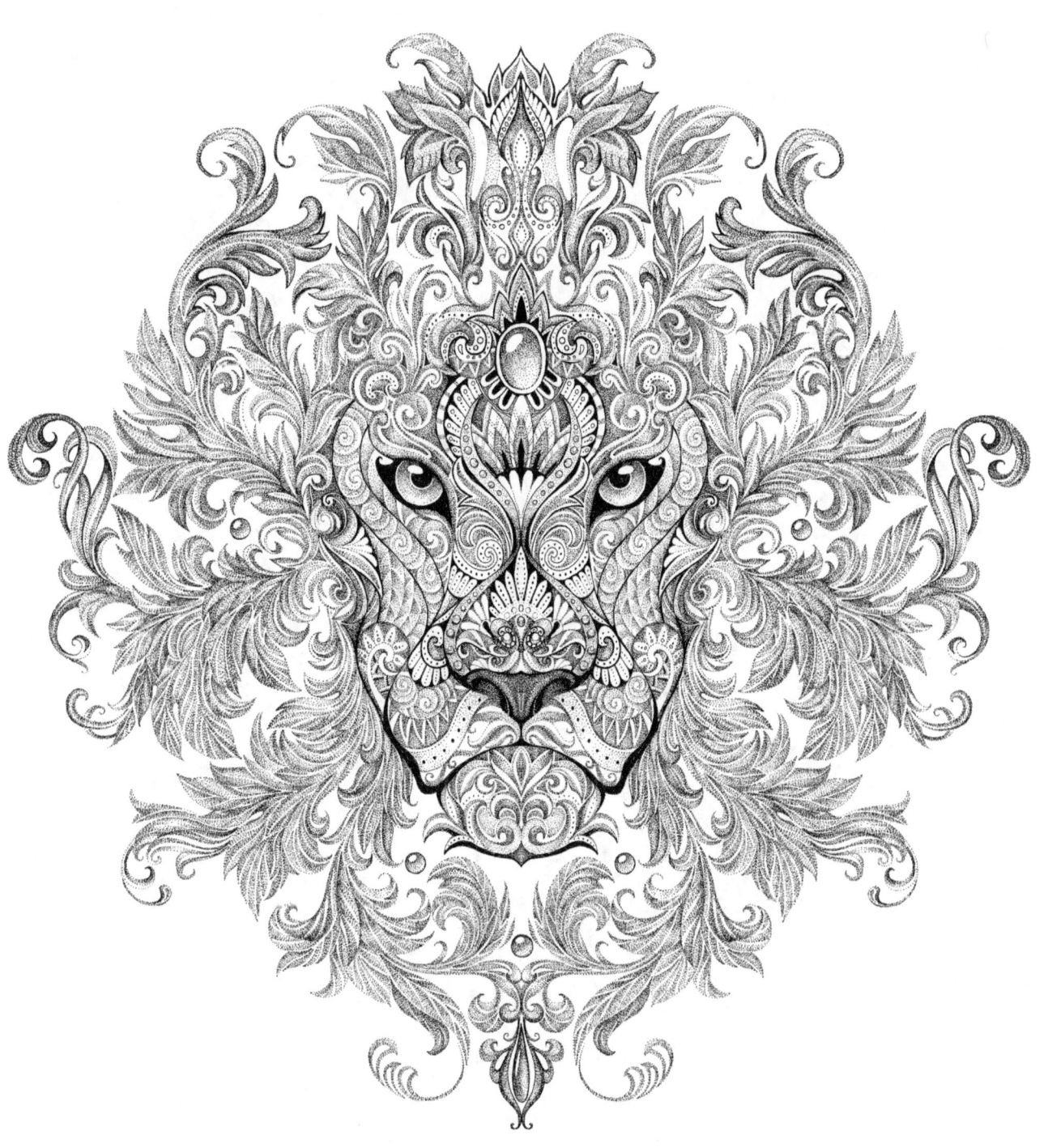

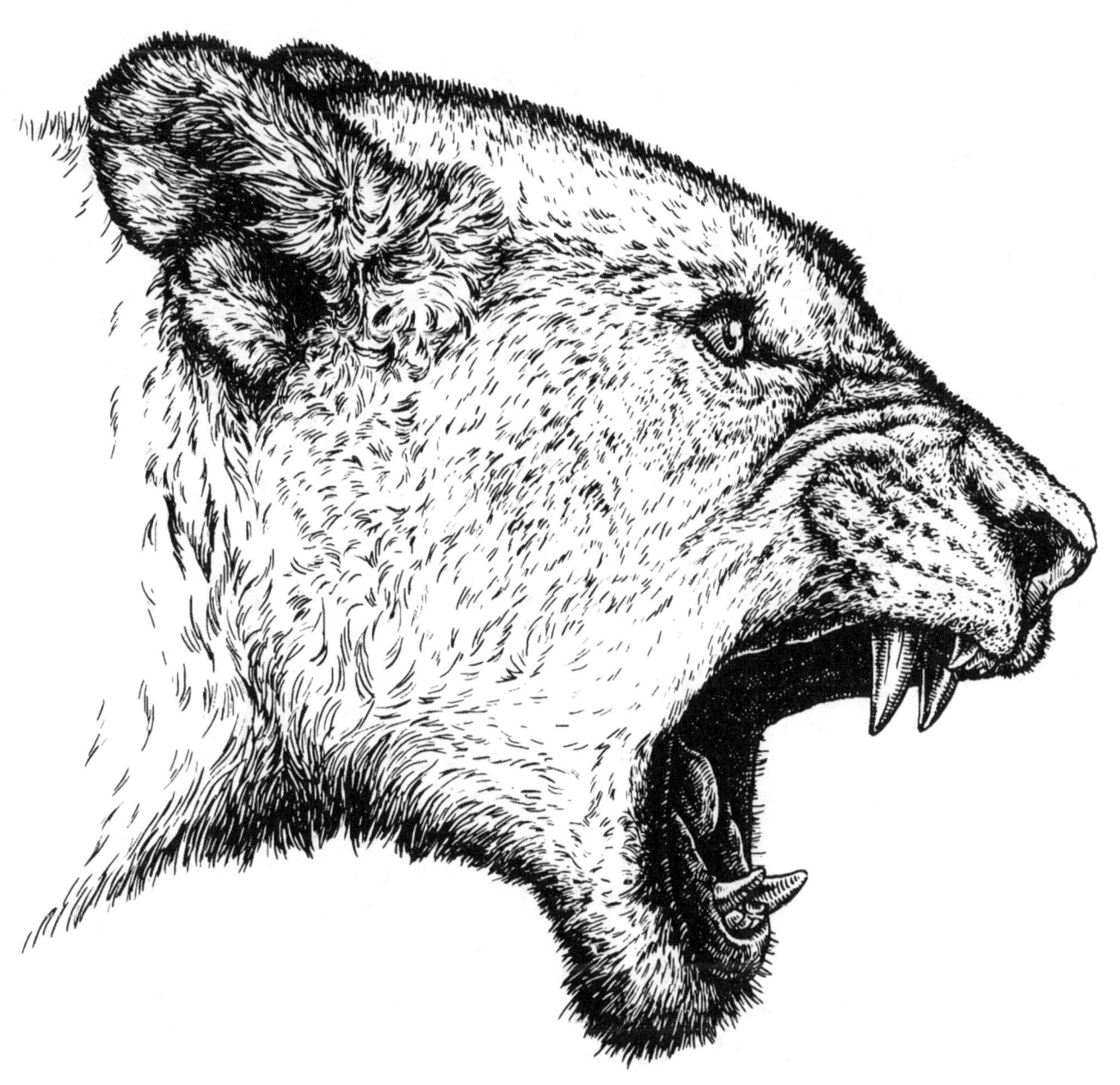

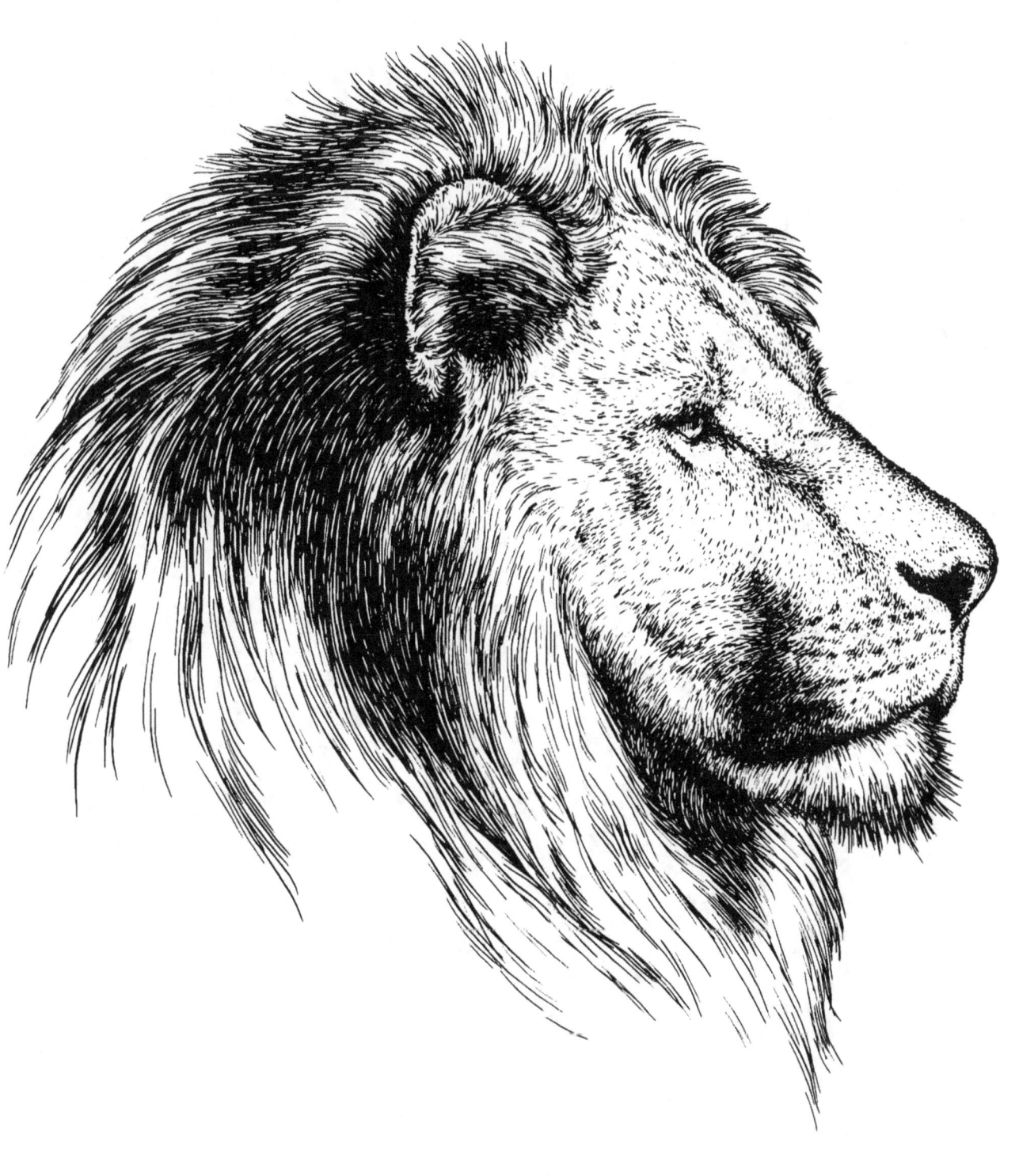

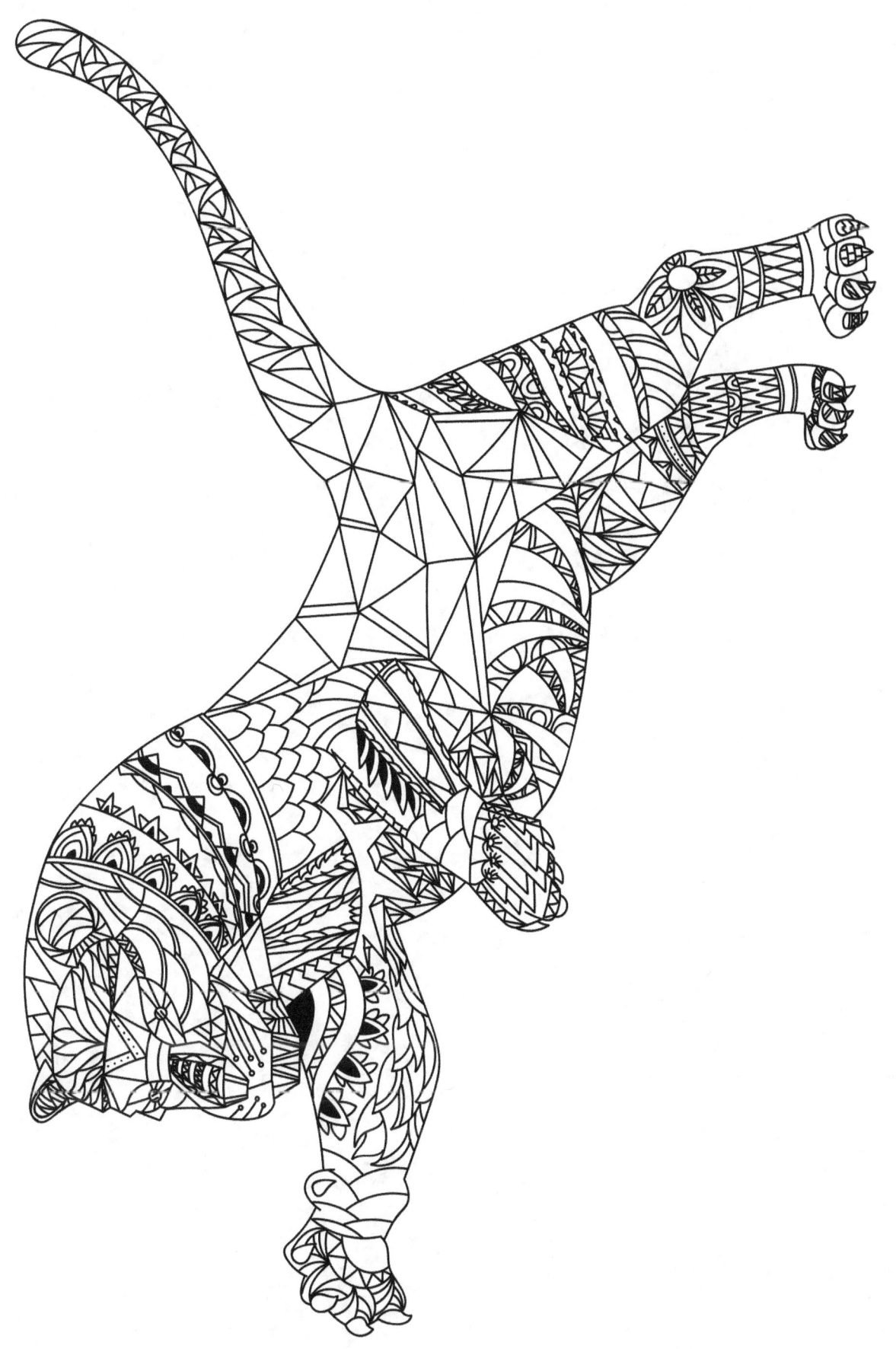

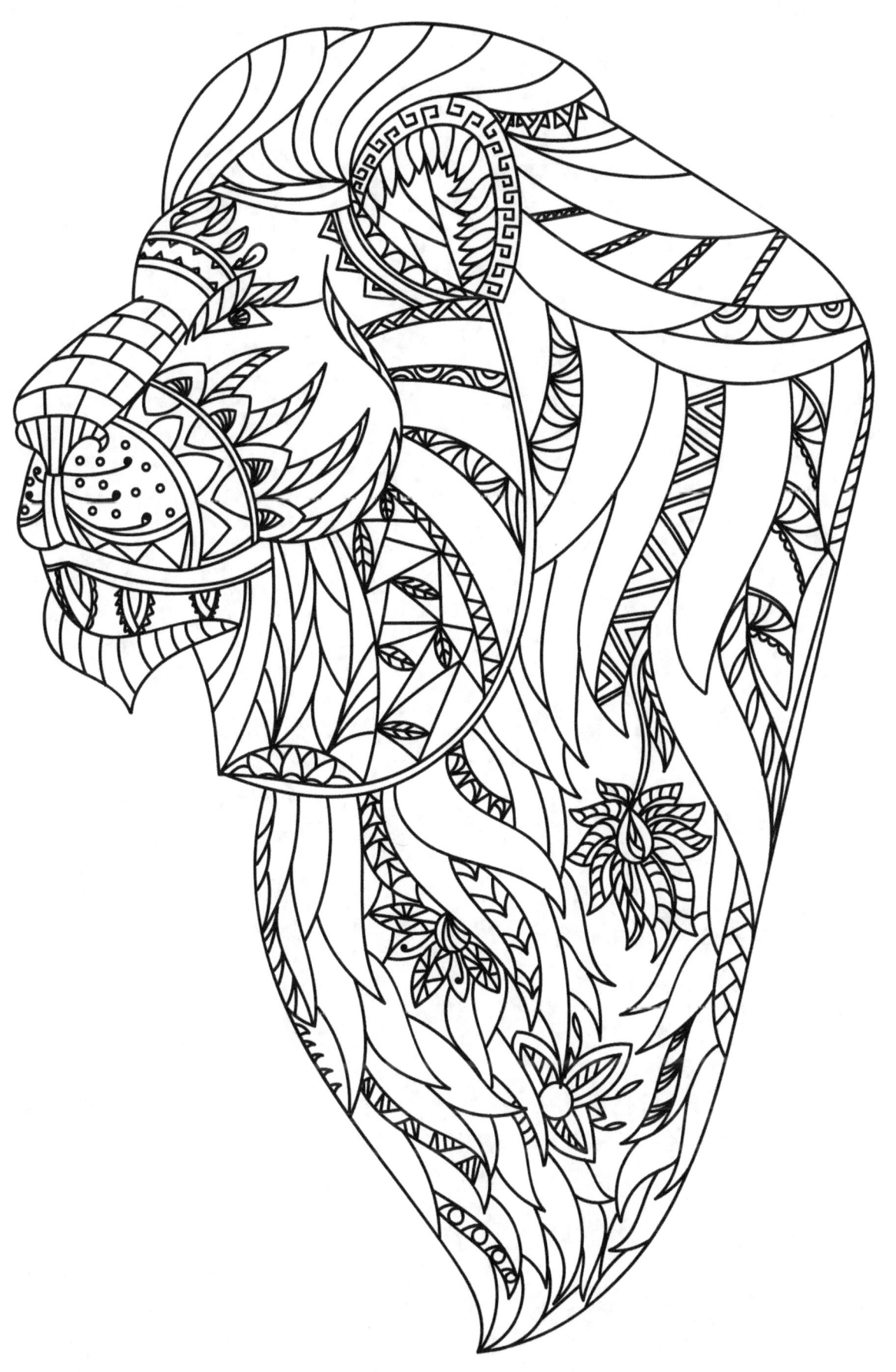